I Am A True Son

By Jonathan Devon Bryant, Sr.

Copyright 2020 by Jonathan D. Bryant, Sr. All rights reserved. This book is protected under the copyright laws of the United States of America and may not be copied or reprinted for commercial gain or profit.

ISBN: 978-1-7360647-0-2

Requests for permissions should be directed to:

Pastor Jonathan Bryant

Cr200 Middleburg Fl. 32068

About the Author

Pastor Jonathan Bryant is the founder, Pastor and a teacher of Faith Outreach Church-FL, a vibrant, non-denominational Spirit-filled Church that for over thirteen years has been called to touch and transform individuals, families and the community with the love and power of Jesus Christ.

The core of Pastor Jonathan's spiritual being and the person he has become is a direct result from the influence and teaching he has received from his Spiritual Parents of the Gospel, Bishop Richard and Pastor Janice Peoples of Faith Outreach Church in Martinez and Hepzibah, GA.

Pastor Jonathan is devotedly married to Stephanie Bryant, with whom he pastors Faith Outreach Church-FL. They have three beautiful children; Jaleesha, Jonathan II, JaRhonda and one grandchild Amari Bradley.

A retired Chief Warrant Officer Three (CW3) with over 20 years of service to the United States Army, Pastor Jonathan has traveled extensively and been given the opportunity to sit under some great men and women of God. He is fondly referred to as "The Original Facebook Pastor", and is a Spiritual Father and mentor to many.

A believer in education, Pastor Jonathan holds an Associates of Arts Degree, Bachelors in Biblical Studies, a Bachelors of Science in (Business and Psychology) from Liberty University and a Masters of Arts in Religion with a prominence in Church Ministries from Liberty Theological Seminary. His studies included dynamic leadership theories, exegetical teaching, methodologies and concepts that seek to create, develop, and sustain believers without compromising the scriptures, as he holds expository preaching in the highest regard.

Pastor Jonathan has a sincere desire to teach and impart a genuine love and appreciation for God's Word into disciples who will help to shape and influence the minds and hearts of all people.

Faith Outreach Church-FL's vision is "To deliberately pursue enfold and develop dynamic disciples through discipline and duplication." (Matthew 28:19-20) Additionally, the vision is to impart faith through teaching and preaching so that the body of Christ will come into the fulfillment of Ephesians 4:13 – that is for the Body of Christ to come to the unity of faith moving rhythmically and easily with each other, efficient and graceful in response to God's Son, fully mature adults, fully developed within and without, fully alive like Christ.

Dedication

My heart spills over with thanks to God for the way He continually empowers me, and to our Lord Jesus, the Anointed One, who found me trustworthy and who authorized me to be his partner in this ministry. (1 Timothy 1:12 TPT)

My deepest appreciation to...

My wife Stephanie M. Bryant, the mother of all my babies, for her love and support throughout my life, ministry, and the writing of this book. She alone knew how important this project was for me both personally and professionally, allowing me the opportunity to spend the necessary hours to put together this book. She offered nothing but encouragement during a very challenging time in our lives. I am eternally grateful to Jesus for the privilege and honor of being married to you since 1991. Thanks be unto you for the hours of editing you contributed to this book. I Love You Gurl Friend. Shucks!

To my children, Jaleesha (Princess), Jonathan II (Jon Boy), JaRhonda (Sunshine) and my grandson Amari Jonathan Bradley (AJ). Thank you for your continued support of the Work of Christ in my life and ministry. I pray each one of you lives the John 10:10 life that Jesus came to give you. Nothing I do can be more of an accomplishment than imparting into your lives and loving your mother. I love you all.

To my spiritual parents Mom and Dad, my wife and I are the fruit of y'all labor. Mom and Dad, we are so thankful for our relationship. We are forever grateful for your dedication to God and your continued rich deposits in our lives. Some people avoid the relationship of spiritual mothers and fathers because of fear of control or manipulation. But when it functions healthily, this relationship is truly a gift from God for our growth and health as believers. It's true that some Spiritual Sons and Spiritual Daughters only want blessings, not correction and guidance by loving spiritual parents. Welp, that is not me, I welcome it no ma'am and no sir I do not like being corrected, but it is what helps me to improve and grow as a true Spiritual Son. I believe that as a true son I've been able to handle correction properly. Mom and Dad, I Love You Big Time!

To my ace boon coon in da hole Pastors Adam and Nervia Morrison of Faith Outreach Church International. Wow, thanks for being more than just friends and covenant family to the Bryant family. My children by their own choosing have always considered you to be their Uncle and Aunt. Thanks for listen to my ups and downs with writing this book, as well as your golden nuggets from time to time. You both truly rejoice at the success of others. We love you all tremendously and Rev, you make the best Sweet Potato Souffle on this side of the dirt. Shucks! Love y'all more than words could express.

To my spiritual sons and daughters. I pray that my wife and I continue to set the right example before you and that this book will help take our relationship to another dimension. Love Always, Dad

To Yuri L. Robinson Photography...Thanks Puma! Love You Sir!

To the entire Faith Outreach Church-Florida who have labored with us and been so supportive of our ministry gift. Thanks! Pastor Love You! #Shucks

In memory of my biological mother who is now in glory. Bessie Lena Battle Tucker. Of course, I have to thank my Mother because...well, she's my Mother! My only regret is that I can't hand my mother a copy of this book and see the look of pride in her eyes.

Love You Mother!

07/29/1950 through 11/03/2015

Foreword

I Am A True Son is a powerful work of art that will challenge you to take an honest look at yourself and your history of true faithfulness and success. If anyone knows how to make and teach the journey from a spiritual son's perspective, Jonathan Bryant is that one.

From day one, as a soldier in the U.S. Army in 1995, this young man and I connected, and we have been joined ever since. If he has ever disagreed or had a problem within our relationship, I would have never known. He has never given me a reason to question his loyalty, commitment, faithfulness, and respect for my position in his life or me as a man.

Through Jonathan Bryant's integrity and humility as a son in the Gospel, he has established a legacy of honor, influence, and sound moral character for others to follow. His life of extraordinary exploits and integrity provides an example of a life dedicated and skilled in the art of "follow-ship". As a spiritual son and as a Pastor, he establishes a standard that is worth studying and following.

We all must recognize the value of fatherhood, not only natural but spiritual as well. There is a deposit, an investment that fathers make that enables sons and daughters to avoid the dysfunctions that have damaged so many young men, women, pastors, ministers, and other leaders. The worst thing a spiritual father can do is leave the scene without allowing his sons and daughters to tap into the anointing on his life; to receive the seed of his spiritual loins. The worst thing a spiritual son or daughter can do is to refuse or reject that opportunity from a spiritual father. In 25 years, Pastor Jonathan Bryant has never rejected the chance to receive, learn, and grow as a student of the Word of God and as a faithful son in this ministry.

Paul refers to himself as a father to the Corinthians, and indirectly pronounces his spiritual fatherhood over Timothy and Titus. *"I am not trying to make you feel ashamed. I am writing this to give you a warning as my own dear children. For though you may have ten thousand teachers in Christ, you do not have many fathers. Through the Good News I became your father in Christ Jesus, so I beg you, please follow my example. That is why I am sending to you Timothy, my son in the Lord. I love Timothy, and he is faithful. He will help you remember my way of life in Christ Jesus, just as I teach it in all the churches everywhere."* (1 Corinthians 4:14-17 NCV)

With great honor and pride, I refer to myself as the spiritual father of my son, Jonathan Bryant. I love this young man, and he is faithful to help others remember the way of life in Christ Jesus. *I Am a True Son* is a book that God has recently given his hands to write; however, the words, the truth, and the wisdom, I have witnessed God as He has been writing these on Jonathan's heart for more than 25 years.

As spiritual fathers, we should never attempt to replace the authority of Scriptures. Our words on earth are simply to confirm what God in Heaven is speaking and to bring peace to our sons and daughters. With that thought, I confirm, this book could not have been written with the same passion, zeal, and honesty if this son did not write it.

Pastors, everyone in your ministry, will not be a son or daughter to you, but you will know those who truly are, and they will know you and who you are in their lives. There will be a covenant connection that miles, years, and growth will only strengthen. You will witness your value in the ministry and family of your spiritual sons and daughters. You will also recognize the difference and impact they make in your ministry and family. *Jonathan, you are my true son in the faith.* I can see the results of our covenant in your ministry. I see and feel the place I have in the life of your family. Your wife, Stephanie is just as committed and faithful to our connection. She is not only your wife; she is my daughter. Your children Jaleesha, Jonathan, and JaRhonda make it clear I am their grandfather, and they value my spiritual presence in their life.

To every spiritual father, every son, and every daughter, as you open the pages of this man's life, prepare to learn through laughter and tears from one who has been called, anointed, and appointed for this assignment in this season: Pastor Jonathan Bryant, Sr., A True Son.
Bishop Richard B. Peoples, Sr. Senior Pastor, Faith Outreach Church & Proud Spiritual Father of the Author of I Am a True Son

To my true son, Jonathan Bryant, Sr., I want to say so many things, but I'm not here to write a book. However, I could when I think of how much I love and appreciate you. Since the start, you have been with us, more than 25 years, and you truly have our heart.

You are sold out for Christ! I have watched you serve from the parking lot to the back door and in the pulpit. You are and have always been dedicated, committed, and tied into the assignment God has on your life. Your life is an illustration of covenant as God intended; a lifelong relationship. Jonathan, all that you do gives testimony that you are an excellent example of what it means to be a spiritual son.

This phenomenal book, *I Am A True Son*, that has been birthed through your life experiences and your walk in Christ is definitely going to impact the Kingdom of God positively. Many do no understand the value of sonship, however, through your willingness to honestly share and reveal all that God has taught you, every reader will have an opportunity to learn. Continue to soar son. We love you, Stephanie, the children, and the family of Faith Outreach Church - Florida! – Mom aka **Dr. Janice E. Peoples, Pastor, Faith Outreach Church**

This Book, "A True Son", is "UNPARALLELED" to any other manuscripts dealing with the subject of Spiritual Fathers and Spiritual Mothers. If you don't throw this book WHILE you are reading it, I'll refund you myself... ShhooT.

I am an eye witness to the life of this Author, Father and Husband of this great book. I have seen his life progress spiritually as a Brother in Christ, Deacon, Minister, Elder, Pastor, Spiritual Father and consistent and un-severed fellowship, as a Spiritual Son, to his Spiritual Father and Mother, Bishop Richard B. Peoples and Dr. Janice Peoples. It has been my honor to submit to his leadership since 1996 #UnBroken!

There is a clarion call in the Body of Christ to BIRTH healthy Sons and Daughters in ministry; and the only vessel QUALIFIED to birth healthy Spiritual Sons and Spiritual Daughters (watch it now) are

#HealthySpiritualFathersAndMothers...ShhooT!

There is much confusion in the Body of Christ of what it means to be a Pastor, Mentor, or Spiritual Father and Spiritual Mother; and unfortunately, many have mistaken the difference, operated in error and has brought much frustration and disappointment upon themselves and most importantly caused spiritual and relational damage to sheep and lambs within their flock.

This Book is a compilation of real life experiences shared from the perspective of someone who is a Pastor, who is a Mentor, who is a Spiritual Father and who is a Bonafide spiritual Son (watch this) and who has, over the years, been given insight under the inspiration of the Holy Spirit to know the difference in the aforementioned spiritual roles.

Within the pages of this book, first of all, you will receive impartation, revelation, spiritual insight and practical wisdom like you have never seen before, hidden in the pages of the B-I-B-L-E relating to Spiritual Parenting.

You will then be able to connect with the thoughts, feelings, and emotions of Pastor Bryant as he imparts his own experiences, detailing how they have affected, effected and impacted the way he approached various situations in ministry. You will experience his struggles and triumphs—and in turn glean some great life application principles that will be beneficial to your growth as a leader of people in ministry.

Pastor Jonathan Bryant is the 'Epitome' of a Spiritual Father and Spiritual Son. He exemplifies CONSISTENT honor and submission as a Spiritual Son and models wisdom, character and spiritual discernment commensurate to his identity as a Spiritual Son to his Spiritual Father and Spiritual Mother.

A great Spiritual parent (watch this) will ensure you leave this life empty. The Book declares in Proverbs 20:5 VOICE, "The real motives come from deep within a person—as from deep waters— but a discerning person is able to draw them up and expose them."

That verse is indicative of the Author of this great manuscript... Pastor Jonathan Devon Bryant ..."The Man"... "The Father"..."The Pastor"..."The Husband"... "The Brother"... "The Son"... "The Mentor"..."The Spiritual Son"..."The Community Leader"... "The Pastor"... "The Covenant Brother"... "The Spiritual Father"... "The Veteran"... "The Servant Leader"

I "Beseech" you, I urge you, to purchase several copies of this book; read it, meditate in it, observe the real life experiences and listen to the spiritual wisdom in the words of this great man; and then put it into practice. ShhooT~ShhuckZ.

Pastors Adam L. Morrison IV and Nervia Morrison. Faith Outreach Church International

Contents

About The Author 03
Dedication 05
Foreword 08
Introduction/Preface 17

Chapter 1 A True Spiritual Son 19
Chapter 2 There Is a Difference Between Pastor,
           Mentor, and Spiritual Parents 37
Chapter 3 Who's The Seeker? 55
Chapter 4 More than Filling out Forms and Giving
           Financial Support 65
Chapter 5 Spiritual Abuse vs Spiritual Correction 75
Chapter 6 Go Purchase Your Parents a Knife 95
Chapter 7 I Have Been Mutilated 113
Chapter 8 Childhood Before Parenthood 131
Chapter 9 Only the Qualified Should Touch You 145
Chapter 10 Accepting the Spiritual Father But
            Rejecting the Spiritual Mother 159
Chapter 11 Like Father, Like Son 177
Chapter 12 Tell Your Feelings How to Feel 201
Chapter 13 Never Expose Your Spiritual Parents 211
Chapter 14 Never Divorce Your Spiritual Parents 221

Conclusion 231

Introduction/Preface

As we journey through the pages of this book, I will develop aspects of what it means to be a spiritual father — and what it does not. Know that my goal is to encourage you in light of God's Word to live as who He called you to be — nothing more and nothing less. The use of the term fathers and sons in this book is not meant in any way to disparage or deny the powerful roles that mothers and daughters fulfill in the Kingdom of God. The principles of ministry are true regardless of gender. It is both "your sons and daughters" who shall prophesy (Joel 2:28) The enemy has worked persistently to produce a feeling of misplacement among those whose church and ministry gift have been tainted with a feeling of illegitimacy.

Trust Him no matter your role in the lives of those around you. Perhaps you are at a stage of life where you are both a spiritual son and a spiritual father. Use this book to help you understand your role in each relationship (and as you pastor your flock and parent your biological children). I have taken this journey — and continue doing so every day. I know many of the pitfalls along the way and hope to steer you through many of the dangers, questions, and pain points along the way. It's my sincere prayer that the succeeding pages of this book prove to effect organizational realignment in the Body of Christ and heal the weeping lacerations of spiritual abuse by showing proper use of spiritual parents' authority and the honor of spiritual sons and daughters. All to the glory of God.

Let's take this journey together, Ahhh Shucks Boy!

Chapter 1

I Am A True Son

The number of children growing up without fathers is massive, and the impact of this on our society is atrocious. The world and the church has been largely ignorant of the full ramifications of this tragedy because we are (Hosea4:6) about the purpose and the value of fatherhood.

Fatherhood and sonship are closely tied together. One cannot be a father without someone to be a father to. While it is possible to be a father to daughters, there is a difference between the relationship fathers have with their daughters and the relationship between a father and a son. Sons bring out something in a father that daughters don't, because the father is an example to his sons in a way that he isn't to his daughters.

Likewise, sons need their fathers. A boy cannot learn how to become a man from a woman. This lesson has been made imminently clear by the high number of single mothers trying to raise their sons in our society today. Those sons will seek out a male role model to follow, unfortunately, often the wrong sort of role model. Rather than finding someone who can teach them how to be a real man, who provides and protects, they find a role model who teaches them how to be a "macho man" and who abuses and takes what he wants.

We see the results of wrong role models when looking at the criminal justice system. Boys raised in a home without a father are twenty times more likely to end up in prison, with 80% of all prison inmates coming from fatherless homes. This isn't an indictment on women, but instead an indication of how much growing boys need their fathers.

However, for a son to receive the benefit of having a father, he must also be a true son. This fact is true both in the spiritual sense and the natural one. Just as a natural son needs to receive instruction and an example from his father, so too a spiritual son needs to receive those things from his spiritual father. But neither son can receive the father's guidance while they are busy walking in rebellion. Their rebellious attitude will block their ability to see the value in the teaching and example their father has to offer them.

In the Bible, Paul refers to Timothy as his true son, addressing his first letter to him by saying:

> *To Timothy, my true son in the faith: Grace, mercy and peace from God the Father and Christ Jesus our Lord.*
>
> *(1 Timothy 1:2)*

Obviously, Paul understood the difference between a "true son" and any other sort of son. That would include false sons, bad sons, and just plain mediocre sons. But what is a "true son"? How can we tell if we are or aren't one? Do we have a good definition or an example? Just what is a true son?

Fortunately, we can find examples of both true sons and bad sons in the Bible, giving us the foundation that we can use to create our own definition. To find them, we will need to look no further than the lives of Elijah and Elisha, one of the more interesting relationships in the Old Testament.

God directed Elijah to anoint Elisha to take his place as prophet after Elijah's ministry came to an end. So we find Elijah obeying God and doing this at the end of 1 Kings 19.

> *So Elijah went from there and found Elisha son of Shaphat. He was plowing with twelve yoke of oxen, and he himself was driving the twelfth pair. Elijah went up to him and threw his cloak around him. Elisha then left his oxen and ran after Elijah. "Let me kiss my father and mother good-by," he said, "and then I will come with you." "Go back," Elijah replied, "What have I done to you?"*
>
> *(1 Kings 19:19-20)*

The church today has become accustomed to the idea of anointing with oil, but apparently, there were other methods used in biblical times. There is no mention of oil in this passage, but Elisha clearly understood the significance of Elijah throwing his cloak over him. He responded immediately to the call.

The "cloak" referred to here was probably Elijah's prayer shawl. That's the way it is understood by the Jewish people, and referenced in their writings. If it was not a prayer shawl, it was some other similar garment specific to prophets and is significant because Elijah was a prophet. Perhaps there was some sort of "prophet's robe" that we are unaware of today, but was known at that time.

Elisha wouldn't have reacted the way he did if he didn't understand the significance of Elijah's actions. It is doubtful that he would have followed a traveling merchant who had thrown his cloak over his shoulders. Elisha came from a wealthy family, as we can see from verse 19, referencing that he was *"plowing with twelve yoke of oxen, and he himself was driving the twelfth pair."* Apparently he was functioning as an overseer of the plowing on his family's farm, with the other oxen being driven by servants. By driving the last pair, he would be in a good vantage point to keep his eye on the entire team.

The quick response of Elisha was not lost upon the prophet. Yet Elijah decided that another test was in order. Perhaps he was concerned because Elisha came from a wealthy family or perhaps it was his nature to test those who he would take as his spiritual son. Either way, Elijah tries to send Elisha back, saying (perhaps even somewhat scornfully), "What have I done to you?"

Yet Elisha passed this test, running back to celebrate with his servants, feeding them of the oxen he had been plowing with. Then the scripture tells us,

> *"He set out to follow Elijah and became his attendant"* (some translations say *"servant"*)
>
> (1 Kings 19:21)

There is little mentioned in the scriptures about what happened between that point in time and Elijah's last day on Earth. However, we know from Jewish history that disciples of rabbis (teachers) would go live with them, as if they were adopted sons, while studying under their tutelage. The same can be applied in this situation, as Elijah was a spiritual father to Elisha, preparing him to take over the office of prophet when Elijah's own time was through, as God had directed him.

During that time, Elisha attended to Elijah, functioning as a servant and freeing his spiritual father of time-wasting details, so that he could concentrate on prayer and his ministry. When Elijah had a need to go out and minister in some capacity, he likely took Elisha along, acting as his assistant, so that Elisha could learn from his example. At times, he may even have had Elisha pray for people or answer their questions and concerns, as part of his training.

Leaving that aside, the next time we see the two of them mentioned together in Scripture is in 2 Kings, 2. This is Elijah's last day on Earth, before the flaming chariot takes him up to heaven. As Elijah and Elisha travel along, walking, Elijah says to Elisha three times: *"Stay here, the Lord has sent me to some other place."* Elijah is referencing first to Bethel (2 Kings 2:2), then to Jericho (2 Kings 2:4), and finally to the Jordan (2 Kings 2:6). Each time, Elisha responded, *"As surely as the Lord lives and as you live, I will not leave you"* (2 Kings 2:2,4,6).

Elisha's dedication to Elijah is clearly manifest here. Just in case we're unsure of that, two different companies of prophets approached him, asking, *"Do you know that the Lord is going to take your master from you today?"* (2 Kings 2:3,5). Both times, Elisha answered, *"Yes, I know, but do not speak of it"* (2 Kings 2:3,5).

Clearly Elisha was a good son to Elijah. However, his own servant, Gehazi, a man who might have followed Elisha in the ministry, was not faithful. He was not a true son, but apparently an opportunist who saw his relationship with Elisha as a job or some means for personal gain.

Naaman, the commanding general of the Syrian army, was stricken with leprosy. Having heard from his wife's servant girl, an Israelite, that there was a prophet in Israel who could cure him of his affliction, he received permission from the king to travel there. Arriving in Samaria, he presented himself to King Joram, who was, of course, unable to cure him. Elisha heard of this and sent for Naaman, giving him directions that led to him being cured (2 Kings 5:1–14). Returning to Elisha, Naaman tried to give him a gift, in gratitude for what he had done, yet Elisha refused (2 Kings 5:16–17).

Here is where we see the character of Gehazi come out.

There was clearly some reason why Elisha refused to accept any payment from Naaman, even though Scripture doesn't give us the reason as to why. Not only does Scripture hide this reason from us, but apparently Elisha hid it from his servant as well. Perhaps it was a test. If it was, Gehazi failed it.

> *After Naaman had traveled some distance, Gehazi, the servant of Elisha the man of God, said to himself, "My master was too easy on Naaman, this Armenian, by not accepting from him what he brought. As surely as the Lord lives, I will run after him and get something from him."*
>
> *(2 Kings 5:19b-20)*

This alone is enough for us to see that Gehazi's heart was not with Elisha. First of all, Gehazi disputed what his master had decided about the gift, without even having any idea of why Elisha declined it. Secondly, it appears that he saw the ministry as a means of receiving money.

The true minister, such as Elisha, ministers because the Lord commanded him to do so, trusting the Lord for financial and material needs. Finally, Gehazi makes a unilateral decision to do something contrary to Elisha's will and doesn't talk to Elisha about it. Had he taken his concerns to Elisha, he might have learned something that would have caused him to act differently.

> *"Is everything all right?" He (Naaman) asked. "Everything is all right," Gehazi answered. "My master sent me to say, 'Two young men from the company of the prophets have just come to me from the hill coun-*

try of Ephraim. Please give them a talent of silver and two sets of clothing."

(2 Kings 5:21-22)

Catching up with Naaman and his company, Gehazi lied, telling him that Elisha had sent him and told a contrived story as justification to ask for money and clothes. Naaman, pleased with his healing, not only gives Gehazi what he asks but doubles the money. He even sends two servants to carry the roughly 150 pounds of silver for Gehazi.

Returning to the house, Gehazi lies to Elisha, apparently thinking he could get away with it. But Elisha sees the lie, either with the help of God or just because he knows his servant. He rebukes Gehazi for his lies and false actions, prophesying to him that Naaman's leprosy would cling to him forever.

Clearly, Gehazi wasn't a true son. In fact, I'd go so far as to say he was a bad son. The surprising thing is that Gehazi was Elisha's servant in the first place. Perhaps his proximity to the prophet was supposed to change his heart and character. If that were so, it appears that Gehazi didn't submit to that part of God's will for his life.

The key difference between Elisha and Gehazi was shown in their relationship with their spiritual fathers. Elisha clearly took every step possible to stay with Elijah, even when he knew that Elijah's time had come. Before the day was out, he would be the one looked to as "the prophet," not just another son of the prophet. His relationship with his spiritual father was more important to him than his own ministry or any other personal gain that might be coming his way.

Unfortunately, that can't be said of Gehazi. While he occupied the same position with Elisha that Elisha had occupied with Elijah, he didn't act as Elisha had done. Rather than being a true son, he was nothing more than a servant, a hired hand. As such, he didn't receive the blessings of a son.

Any true son reflects the character and heart of his father. While he can still have his own personality and desires, his character comes from his relationship with his father. He learns how to be a godly man by following in the footsteps of a godly man.

This is why the whole father/son relationship is so important. Sons can go off to school somewhere and have their heads filled with knowledge, but that doesn't mean that their hearts have been formed into what God wants them to be. Without a godly example to follow and the challenge of truly trying to become like that example, all they get at college is head knowledge, not heart knowledge.

Elisha wasn't just trying to learn how to be a prophet; he was becoming a younger version of Elijah. Not only that, but he was learning how to become more of an Elijah than Elijah himself was. The anointing which ended up resting on Elisha's life was greater than that of Elijah. If we include the man who was brought back to life after being thrown onto Elisha's bones (3 Kings 13:21), there were exactly twice the number of miracles that occurred through Elisha's ministry as there were through Elijah's.

How did this come about? First, as a true son, Elisha was dedicated to Elijah. We've already discussed that. But then, on Elijah's last day on Earth, he asked Elisha what he wanted him to do before he was taken away (2 Kings 2:9). Elisha responded:

> *"Let me inherit a double portion of your spirit."*
> *(2 Kings 2:9)*

Elisha made an interesting request! His request is connected to the number of miracles performed through Elisha's ministry. But there was something else there. Elisha's request shows that he knew who he was and what his relationship to Elijah was. He was asking for the blessing of the firstborn son.

In ancient Israel, the inheritance of a father was broken up between his sons, with the eldest son receiving double what the others received, the "double portion." By asking for this, Elisha was saying that he knew that he had that right of inheritance as the firstborn son. But that's not all. He was also declaring that he knew he was the true spiritual son of Elijah and, therefore, had the right to ask for that blessing.

Others quickly recognized that too. When Elisha returned back across the Jordan River, after Elijah had been taken up by the flaming chariot, the story continues, telling us:

> *The company of the prophets from Jericho, who were watching, said, "The spirit of Elijah is resting on*

Elisha" And they went to meet him and bowed to the ground before him.

(2 Kings 2:15)

True sonship is something that must be visible to others. It isn't enough that the son claims that title for himself. Elijah didn't even have to claim it in this story. The same company of the prophets who told him that Elijah would be taken from him that day, recognized it.

It is interesting to note that the company of the prophets called Elijah "Elisha's master." Obviously, they had seen the two of them together before, and knew of the closeness of their relationship. The prophets had been impacted to some extent by seeing Elijah and Elisha's relationship.

If a son's relationship isn't close enough to his spiritual father for people to comment on it, he must not be a true son. Rather, while he may occupy the position of a son, he is nothing more than a mediocre son. He's someone who is there to see what he can get, ignoring the deeper and more important things his spiritual father might have to offer.

Elisha's commitment to his spiritual father as a true son, led to submission to him as well. For without submission, there is no sonship. We recognize this even in the natural. Sons submit to their fathers, or they find themselves being disciplined. A father who doesn't discipline his son, hates him (Proverbs 13:24). While I would not expect Elijah to turn Elisha over his knee and spank him, there are other ways he would have disciplined him.

Yet, I doubt that there was much need for Elijah to discipline Elisha. True discipline comes from within, from the same place that true submission does, the heart. It appears that Elisha had plenty of that sort of discipline.

We must be clear — submission and subjugation aren't the same thing. When a parent punishes a child, forcing him to obey, the parent is subjugating him. When a child chooses to submit of his own accord, then he is being that true son, who realizes that what his father tells him to do is best for his life.

Those who are merely subjugated, rather than submitted, can be classified as "spiritual enthusiasts" rather than true sons. You see them in the church all the time. They get excited about the presence of God and what God is doing, but they aren't willing to submit and obey what the Word of God tells them to do. They think God's Word isn't true or that some things should change to reflect modern culture. In other words, they want God to change so that they can continue their sinful lifestyle.

Submission is badly misunderstood in today's culture. The world around us looks at those who have submitted and thinks they are weak. They scoff, and say that a "real man" stands on his own two feet. That is merely a reflection of the rebellious society in which we live. People don't want to be accountable to any human authority, so when it comes time to be accountable to God's authority, they don't know how.

Obedience and submission aren't the same thing either, although submission will usually bring about obedience. Nevertheless, it is possible for one to obey, without submitting, as obedience is the external act, while submission is a thing of the heart. Without true submission within the heart, we are like the child who is told to sit in the corner, in punishment. He might go sit there, because he has to, but he could be saying to himself "I may be sitting down on the outside, but I'm standing up on the inside."

For submission to be true submission, it has to reach the point of saying, "Your will is my will, and your desires are my desires." This is what the Lord expects of us, in our relationship with Him. Until we reach that point, we are not fully submitted.

Yet without submission, we can never reflect Christ-likeness in our lives. We will always struggle with wanting our own way. After our salvation, this is the single most important thing that God desires to do in us.

> *For those God foreknew He also predestined to be conformed to the likeness of His Son, that He might be the firstborn among many brother.*
>
> *(Romans 8:29)*

Submitting to an earthly father, whether a natural father or a spiritual one, is an integral part of learning how to submit to our Heavenly Father. Then, and only then, can we receive the fullness of all that He has for us. Without that, we will never see Romans 8:29 fully manifest in our lives.

Had Elisha not fully submitted to Elijah of his own free will, he would not have been in the place of receiving the double portion of Elijah's spirit that he asked for. Yet we know that he did receive that, which tells us that he truly submitted to his spiritual father, as a true son.

Also, not only would Elisha not have received the double portion, but Elijah's covering would not be over him. For anyone who is under such covering, to receive the benefit of their spiritual covering, they must keep themselves under that covering. It's not up to the spiritual father to run around, chasing his spiritual son or daughter, to offer that covering to them. It's up to the son or daughter to stay close to their spiritual father, where they are covered.

We can more easily see this in the natural world. A young son who is running around in a bad neighborhood is going to fall into evil. Whether he commits those evil acts himself because he is coerced into it, or whether some bully commits them against him, he will be harmed by them. But if that same son stays close to his father, he is protected from harm. His father, acting as his covering, will protect him, not allowing those influences in his life. That bully won't push that son because he will recognize that there is a stronger person who is protecting him.

The bad son will only try to use his father to protect him when the bully (devil) appears. He will then run back to his father, standing in his shadow as a safe place. From there, he will taunt the bully, knowing that the bully won't do a thing. Yet as soon as the bully (devil) is gone, he will leave that place of protection, seeking his own will and his own way.

Isn't that what Gehazi did? He was with Elisha when it was convenient for him to be so, but when he saw an opportunity, he went away, seeking what he could get. Because Gehazi chose that, he opened himself up for attack and ended up becoming afflicted by the leprosy of Naaman.

So what exactly is this submission, if it is so important? If we look in the book of Ephesians, we find a Greek word for submission that is very interesting. It says:

> *Wives, **submit** to your husbands, as to the Lord.*
> *(Ephesians 5:22)*

Don't get confused. I'm not switching subjects here. That word "submit" in that verse is the Greek word *huspotasso*. This word doesn't just mean submit as we understand the word today, but also includes the concept of "adapt yourself to."

This is exactly the sort of submission that the Lord is looking for in our lives. As a true son submits himself to a true spiritual father, the father becomes an example of Christ-likeness to his son. So as the son is adapting himself to his father, or becoming like his father, he is also becoming more and more like Christ, *"conformed to the likeness of His Son"* (Romans 8:29). It's an integral part of the process.

The true son wants to become like his father, because he recognizes the value in being like him. In this, he prepares himself to receive all that his father has for him, not so much in the material or financial realms, but in the inner things of the heart, the character of his father. Without the ministry and impartation of a spiritual father's strengths and love, spiritual children can grow up not knowing who they are, why they are here, or where they are going. They grow up at risk of unstableness, insecurity, lack of discipline, lack of motivation and without a sense of personal vision, purpose or destiny.

Let us examine this periciope in order for me to further build and clarify my case. The words which God the Father spoke over His Son on the day that Jesus was baptized and anointed for ministry were, "This is my Son, whom I love: with him I am well pleased" (Matthew 3:17). Here was an affirmation of identity, love, acceptance, blessing, honor and, indirectly, permission to succeed in life and ministry.

The key elements seen here in the periciope: the father gives identity, expresses His love, and declares the delight He has in His son. Everything flows from this, both in natural families and in the spiritual life of the family of God. In fact, Jesus never did any miracles until He received affirmation and confirmation from His father. In the ministry of the church, there are important things that can only come to us through the ministry of spiritual fathers. I beech you by the mercies of God that if you haven't received affirmation or confirmation from your spiritual father you are missing out on another level of greatness that you could be functioning in.

In this, the spiritual son not only becomes like his spiritual father but also receives the ability to go beyond where his spiritual father did. Each generation will grow in the grace of God, becoming more Christ-like and able to accomplish the will of our Heavenly Father here upon the Earth. The anointing power of the Holy Spirit will be increased in his life and, through that, in the church. God's will can then be accomplished in a greater way for His Glory.

Please hear my heart and receive this message, that in the ministry of the church there are important things that can only come to us through the ministry of spiritual fathers. If your heart desires to grow into spiritual maturity and hearing the call of God to the ministry, regardless of your age or gender it will enhance your ministry gift greatly if there is a spiritual father voice in your life, who communicates to you heart love, acceptance, identity, and permission to be a success.

The following biblical description of the spiritual father ministry comes alive for us when we are more informed of the importance of a father's role in our life. In 1 Thessalonians it is written, "*6-8* Even though we had some standing as Christ's apostles, we never threw our weight around or tried to come across as important, with you or anyone else. We weren't aloof with you. We took you just as you were. We were never patronizing, never condescending, but we cared for you the way a mother cares for her children. We loved you dearly. Not content to just pass on the Message, we wanted to give you our hearts. And we *did*.

> *9-12* "*You remember us in those days, friends, working our fingers to the bone, up half the night, moonlighting so you wouldn't have the burden of supporting us while we proclaimed God's Message to you.*

> *You saw with your own eyes how discreet and courteous we were among you, with keen sensitivity to you as fellow believers. And God knows we weren't freeloaders! You experienced it all firsthand. With each of you we were like a father with his child, holding your hand, whispering encouragement, showing you step-by-step how to live well before God, who called us into his own kingdom, into this delightful life."*
>
> *(1 Thessalonians 2:6-12 The Message Bible)*

The bottom line is this. We need spiritual fathers in our lives. Without the appropriate Spirit-appointed covering in our lives we simply cannot flourish and experience the fullness of the Holy Spirit's plans and purposes for our lives or become mature spiritual fathers or spiritual mothers ourselves.

If you don't have the benefit of being covered by a spiritual father, ask the Lord to facilitate that relationship in your life. Begin making it a matter of prayer focus and then be willing to listen and to move in the direction He sets you in.

Amen and Amen!

Chapter 2

There Is a Difference Between a Pastor, Mentor, and Spiritual Parents

You may have 10,000 mentors who work for the Messiah, but not many fathers. For in the Messiah Jesus I became your father through the gospel.

(1 Corinthians 4:15 (International Standard Version)

I know from experience that there is a difference in the function of the three positions of pastor, mentor and spiritual parent because I function in all three of them. Throughout my military career and my Christian walk, I have witnessed first-hand many believers hurt — and still hurting — within the body of Christ because they do not know how to distinguish the difference in the three positions.

They put their hopes in the person in the wrong position, only to be hurt when that person does not meet their expectations. Or the person in a particular position does not have a clear understanding of what he is supposed to do and where to draw the line. Boundaries are broken, and there is pain.

The two main ingredients that I believe are missing in helping believers place the right label on the correct relationship are

1. teaching with understanding
2. godly discernment

I will help you understand both of these missing elements throughout the course of this book.

Once a believer has been taught the scriptures that have been rightly divided, he must spiritually discern whom he should be submitted to as a pastor, mentor, or spiritual parent.

So, without saying, you must be taught the scriptures correctly. There are misunderstandings, misinterpretations, and passages taken out of context that must be dealt with. We will take time to look at the foundational passages about each of these positions in context so that we can understand them correctly.

Then, we will use biblical examples and relationships to give you insight as you spiritually discern who to submit to as your pastor, mentor, or spiritual parent.

In all your getting, you must get an understanding. The way you gain understanding, is to decide who you will stand under, shucks Pastor.

So, let's begin with a look at these important passages from the Bible so that we understand them in their original contexts.

Note that this first passage is foundational to our book and this teaching. I am including more context here than in the single verse at the beginning of this chapter:

> *I do not write these things to shame you, but to warn and advise you as my beloved children. For even if you were to have ten thousand teachers [to guide you] in Christ, yet you would not have many fathers [who led you to Christ and assumed responsibility for you], for I became your father in Christ Jesus through the good news [of salvation]. So I urge you, be imitators of me [just as a child imitates his father].*
>
> *(1 Corinthians 4:14-16 Amplified Bible)*

Paul writes these words to the Corinthians in the midst of instructions to them about the Christian ministry. As he does in so many of his letters to churches, Paul has clearly described the gospel message and their calling as Christians. He wants them to know who they are and whose they are in Christ before diving into any other topic.

Similarly, I want to make clear that this book is written for Christians. Not that I wouldn't want someone who isn't a believer to pick up this book and learn about God's plan and purpose here on earth, bringing us alongside others to become more like Christ through the trials and tribulations of life. Shucks, that is the reason that I am a pastor, I submitted to the call of God upon my life to preach His Word.

But this is part of God's plan for discipling believers in this way, and for that reason it would not make sense to an unbeliever reading this book in the same way it should to a believer. If you are reading this as a seeker, I encourage you to find a believer you know or pastor who can tell you the full picture of the gospel. Or, please write me at the address on the copyright page of this book. I would love to talk with you!

After Paul addresses the Corinthians, encouraging them in their faith and calling, he discusses their local church. Then in chapter 4, the chapter that contains our focus verses, Paul begins to instruct them about the basic characteristics of the Christian ministry.

Paul begins by focusing on how they should be good stewards. Remember, that is part of what I am saying we need to focus on, how to divide the word of truth correctly, and follow it so that we apply it to our lives as God would have us do.

Paul also instructs them to be humble servants as Jesus had showed them through even his willingness to die on the cross. Pastor, sometimes we forget our humility. We are confident in our preaching skills. We become comfortable in the church where we have been pastoring. Maybe we are satisfied because of our numbers — either the one in the offering plate or the people in the pews on Sundays. We forget that there are so many things we don't know and unseen changes and challenges ahead. We must always approach life with humility in light of our great and mighty God.

In verses 14-16, Paul turns toward the spiritual role of the father in Christian ministry. Paul clearly takes on the differences between spiritual fathers and other spiritual teachers and leaders in these verses. You might have many teachers and mentors but only one father spiritually (as you have only one biologically). The father is a special role in the lives of those who are his children.

Certainly, all the Corinthians were, in a sense, Paul's children in the faith. Acts 18 shows us that this church began through a relationship he formed first with Aquila and Priscilla. Together they were tentmakers in Corinth. This stop in Paul's missionary journey was not one of the quick ones. Acts 18 shows us that Paul stayed in Corinth for 18 months, preaching the gospel. Silas and Timothy joined him there, in fact, so he could focus more completely on delivering the gospel message.

We don't know how long Paul labored before the conversions began to happen, but the Bible tells us that Paul "devoted himself exclusively to preaching, testifying to the Jews that Jesus was the Christ." He was weekly, on the Sabbath, preaching Jesus in the synagogue, reasoning with Jews about the gospel — even to the point of being persecuted. Paul, in fact, left the temple because of the abuse he suffered.

Many would have given up at this point. Let's face it, pastor. None of us like to be opposed. None of us like conflict. None of us like to be treated unjustly. Our culture would say, just move on. There's always another neighborhood, another church, another city, another person down the road somewhere else. We too often quit in the face of hardship.

Paul may have left the synagogue, but he landed next door! He began to preach to both Jews and Gentiles. In this persecution, the synagogue ruler and his entire family came to believe. Many Corinthians came to believe and were baptized because of Paul's preaching. After that time was up, Paul moved on to Ephesus, but he obviously kept up with them, following reports, and writing letters to them afterwards.

So, Paul helped deliver the Christian message to those who he had written to, the first generation Christians of Corinth and those they had shared the gospel with after he left. In this sense, he is like a father who stands by his spouse in the delivery room. He was there from the birth of the Corinthian church, playing a special role in their spiritual birth.

This spiritual connection gives Paul a special precedence that no other could have. That connection gives him the authority and right to ask the Corinthians to imitate him in following Christ. He, as their spiritual parent, disciplined (that is, taught) through encouragement and chastisement as necessary to help them stay on the right path. It is clear throughout Corinthians that Paul did not take it easy on them. In fact, he even alludes to another letter that was particularly corrective on their behavior — but it is the right and duty a father has to exercise.

Paul earned this respect further through his perseverance and through persecution. He also did not rely on their support for his ministry. Paul earned his living and support as a tentmaker. He knew that many charlatans in the church only cared about money and lived on the support of others. Paul would not have any of that.

All of this is why Paul explains later about his request to imitate him in 1 Corinthians 11:1, "Be followers of me as I follow Christ." Paul is not exalting himself but always points to Jesus as the author and finisher of their faith. He is looking for their maturity — the same goals that he has personally. They are on this journey together, running the race and getting others to join them in the journey.

Like many people, the Corinthians did not need to be told alone, but also to be shown. Paul taught the faith, but he lived it out passionately in the pursuit of following Christ. The Corinthians needed both word and example in growing into mature Christians.

Paul also demonstrated the time it took to teach children as fathers do. He visited them in person and through letters. He sent messengers and co-laborers to help when he could not be physically present. He poured over them in prayer before God. A spiritual parent is much like a biological one. You are always "on," and need to be ready in an instant to jump into action, and need to pour your life into your child.

Let's take a look at another relationship that highlights what Paul meant for a spiritual father to be — Timothy.

> *"To Timothy my true son in the faith."*
> *(1 Timothy 1:2 New International Version)*

Paul's relationship with Timothy takes the example of a spiritual father a step further. Timothy, like the Corinthians, was a special part of Paul's ministry. However, when Paul met him, Timothy was already a believer (Acts 16) and recommended by the leaders of the church who spoke well of him.

But Paul took him under his wing and called him into the gospel ministry. Paul appointed Timothy to pastor the local congregation in Ephesus. Paul and Timothy served as co-laborers on many missionary journeys. Timothy was with Paul in Corinth as well. Paul oftentimes sent Timothy as his ambassador to minister to those he cared about. Timothy was as much a partner in ministry as Paul could have, but as we shall see, one who needed a spiritual father.

Timothy perhaps needed Paul even more because his own father was a Greek. It was his mother and grandmother who taught him the scriptures from an early age, not his father. As far as we know, Timothy did not have a spiritual father in his life at any point — just the pastor and mentors growing up in the local church in this region of Derbe, Lystra, and Iconium.

Because of the aspects of this story, Timothy also illustrates the special role that parents have in raising children and how a spiritual father is different. Timothy's mother and grandmother were Jews and taught him the Scriptures. They gave him the foundation upon which his faith was founded. But, it was Paul that affirmed Timothy of his calling from God and gave him his first opportunity to serve on mission for God.

Paul reminded Timothy of that mission often. From the tone of Paul's letters to Timothy, Timothy must have gotten discouraged in his ministry and perhaps also in his personal health. Paul encouraged him to stay on there at Ephesus and finish his work (1 Tim. 1:3) and not to let other discourage him because of his youth (1 Tim. 4:12; 2 Tim. 2:6-8). These were challenges that Timothy faced throughout his ministry at Ephesus.

Paul's letters also show us that he encouraged Timothy to preach God's Word and stand strong in it. You will note that this is a common theme in the letters to Timothy and Corinth — always pointing to God and His Word. Paul never builds himself up but encourages godly discipleship (becoming more like Christ).

2 Timothy contains many of the same themes that 1 Timothy does, but notice the love that pours out of Paul's heart for Timothy in 2 Timothy 1. In his first letter, Paul called Timothy "my own son in the faith." In 2 Timothy, Paul calls him "my dearly beloved son."

Time and trials in the ministry together had brought them closer together. How? 2 Timothy 1:3-4 show us the heart of Paul through the prayers he prayed for Timothy. Many of us may think of being a spiritual father as offering a lot of advice. Let me challenge that.

What if for every hour we spent in godly conversation with our spiritual son, we spent two hours in prayer for him before our Heavenly Father? That is the heart of a spiritual father. Don't take it lightly!

So what do these passages mean for you, pastor, as you preach the word in your local church. Let's go back to the purpose of this chapter in recognizing the different positions of mentor, pastor, and coach. What are they? And how do you discern the difference?

Let's start with a mentor. Mentoring is for a seasonal time or transitional at best between stages of life or specifically in learning a new skill.

Read Paul's words in 1 Corinthians 4:14-15 again:

> *"I'm not writing these things to make you ashamed but to warn you, since you are my loved children. You may have ten thousand mentors in Christ, but you don't have many fathers. I gave birth to you in Christ Jesus through the gospel."*

The ratio is 10,000 to 1. A mentor in your life might be every Sunday School teacher, Vacation Bible School leader, choir teacher, missions director, or children's church worker you ever had. They led you for a season. Sometimes there are mentoring moments that stand out in what you learned for a specific moment in time. For this reason, your mentors may also be your coaches, schoolteachers, neighbors, or even friends' parents. Connections may be more loose and casual.

Just because someone mentors you, does not mean they are your spiritual father or spiritual mother of the gospel of Jesus Christ. If you're mis-labeling the relationship after reading this chapter, fix it immediately. You should *never* expect a mentor to give you something that was only intended to come through your spiritual parents.

When someone is mentoring you, it's usually centered around a spiritual goal, or a specific skill set, such as sermon preparation or music lessons. Musicality is "sensitivity to, knowledge of, or talent for music" or "the quality or state of being musical" and is used to refer to "specific, if vaguely defined qualities in pieces and/or genres of music, such as melodiousness and harmoniousness" (Wikipedia).

A mentor can do that without love for you or your family. They are not as invested in you. They may care about the outcome of one event that is a small part of your life. When you have perfected the skill set, the mentor transitions on to the next mentee without a care in the world. That is why you can have 10,000 of them. You can cheat (get insight) on your mentors but please don't cheat on your spiritual parents. 10:000 to 1.

Pastors, please hear my heart on this and learn from my experience. I caused myself and others pain and frustration in ministry because I thought that if people kept coming to my church for months, that they need to join and become a part of the ministry. I took rejection more personally than I should have. I thought we were the best thing around. Why would someone *not* want to join our church?

I mean, who keeps coming to eat from the king's table every Sunday if they did not enjoy the fresh manna (sermon) that was prepared each week? Then it hit me in 2020 that, for some people, I am just 1 of the 10,000 mentors they have. They are there to be mentored and inspired and connect elsewhere. I think somebody just missed that — me.

Pastors, the unnecessary pain and frustration in ministry comes when they (the mentee) join your church and then leave after 3 months. I get it now, because, as a pastor, you invest your time and talent in people. When they get frustrated with something or someone and leave for the megachurch down the street or just give up church altogether, it stings.

They did not really get involved while they were at your church; therefore, it's just easier for them to move on to the next.

Secretly, pastors, you are angry and hurt. Let me encourage your heart, pastor. Many of those people have a vagabond spirit in them, and you were only supposed to mentor them and not become their pastor.

A vagabond spirit is a person who wanders from place to place or church hops. They live an irregular or an aimless wandering life. Our world encourages that today. I hear parents telling what activities their children are involved in — sports, music lessons, ballet, etc. — and church is just one of a long list of things. It does not have a higher priority for most families. In fact, it is more difficult even to expect every family to be there every Sunday morning.

Think about this verse first spoken to Cain by God:

> *"You will always travel from place to place on the earth."*

(Genesis 4:12 (New Life Version)

The vagabond spirit is upon those who are impatient; therefore, they cannot just wait upon God. Think about Cain: when his offering was rejected, what other options did he have aside from anger and jealousy directed toward Abel? He took it personally.

What if he had said instead: "God, what do you want me to learn through this lesson?" or "What did I do wrong?"

How many of us go through life so focused on how much people approve of us or like us, rather than taking each opportunity of every moment we have with them? The first thought is selfish. The second realizes how fleeting life is, and that you should take the most of every opportunity.

Those with the vagabond spirit want to go from place to place, without truly seeking God's will in prayer. Cain had an opportunity to repent, but he did not. God wanted him to stop his restlessness and find a home in Him. God forgave Adam and Eve. God would have done the same for Cain had he repented.

The vagabond spirit refuses and rejects transparency and authentic accountability that comes along with being a congregant. They excuse themselves by saying things like: "The Lord said to me that I should keep moving." Their restlessness gives away their lack of peace and contentment. They lack the life's purpose and calling that God desires we have.

But the question to them is: "You think God wants you to

keep moving? Into what exactly?" If you dare, you might ask: "Are you moving or are your *running*?"

That sheep (person) was not your assignment to pastor but to mentor. Just because they come to your church does not mean you are their pastor.

Hello somebody, Pastor, your assignment was to be 1 of the 10,000 mentors — nothing more and nothing less.

You have to mature in ministry and be okay with that. Likewise, Pastor, just because you pastor someone does not mean that person is your spiritual son or daughter.

Shucks, congregant, listen to me. You will continue to miss out if you do not discern what the Spirit is saying to you. It might be fine to have all three of these figures in your life: a mentor, a pastor, and spiritual parents.

But don't get them confused. Again, your mentor is more like someone who trains and guides you at your work. Think of it more as an apprentice position where you learning a set of tasks or skills.

That relationship is for a time, and then it is gone. You learn the skills, and you do not need the mentor any longer.

Your pastor is like a mentor, but he functions differently. A pastor preaches God's Word. His job is to encourage and challenge you with God's truths in the Bible.

A pastor is also a shepherd, who guides his flocks spiritually. He counsels and advises others spiritually.

Pastors also lead his congregation in some of the most amazing and challenging times of life. He is there when your child is born. He baptizes your child. He marries your child and his spouse.

And he is there in those shadow of the valley of death moments – the worst of times. The pastor is there to remind us of God's Word and will throughout all we experience.

Let's look at the passages that speak into the qualifications of a pastor. First, let's look at Titus 1:6-9:

> *⁶ An elder must be blameless, faithful to his wife, a man whose children believe and are not open to the charge of being wild and disobedient. ⁷ Since an overseer manages God's household, he must be blameless—not overbearing, not quick-tempered, not given to drunkenness, not violent, not pursuing dishonest gain. ⁸ Rather, he must be hospitable, one who loves what is good, who is self-controlled, upright, holy and disciplined. ⁹ He must hold firmly to the trustworthy message as it has been taught, so that he can encourage others by sound doctrine and refute those who oppose it.*

There are many things that this qualification of a pastor does, but who is he? He is an overseer of his flock. A shepherd may have 100 sheep, and he is responsible for taking care of them all. Although he may leave to rescue one who is in trouble, he guides the whole congregation.

How does he guide them? This passage speaks specifically about the pastor holding firmly to the trustworthy message – he preaches the Word of God. He is to encourage the flock with it but also defend the truth for those who try to refute it.

The pastor is a shepherd, proclaimer, prophet, and defender in front of his flock.

Now let's look at 1 Timothy 3:1-7:

> *Here is a trustworthy saying: Whoever aspires to be an overseer desires a noble task. ² Now the overseer is to be above reproach, faithful to his wife, temperate, self-controlled, respectable, hospitable, able to teach, ³ not given to drunkenness, not violent but gentle, not quarrelsome, not a lover of money. ⁴ He must manage his own family well and see that his children obey him, and he must do so in a manner worthy of full respect. ⁵ (If anyone does not know how to manage his own family, how can he take care of God's church?) ⁶ He must not be a recent convert, or he may become conceited and fall under the same judgment as the devil. ⁷ He must also have a good reputation with outsiders, so that he will not fall into disgrace and into the devil's trap.*

Notice that this passage also talks about the pastor's family and managing them well. One might say the same about spiritual children. How can you take care of spiritual children unless you take care of your own at home?

This is more than a casual observation, but is the primary point of the question in verse 5. How can a pastor take care of a church if he can't manage his own family? And he must do so with respect. Pastors, don't let me step on any toes here. But if you are a different person at home behind closed doors with your family than you are behind the pulpit, it is not going to work. The call here is to be authentic in all of your relationships, with your family, with your flock, and with those who are not

Christians. You should be viewed with respect by how you handle yourself.

Let's look next at 1 Peter 5:1-4.

> *To the elders among you, I appeal as a fellow elder and a witness of Christ's sufferings who also will share in the glory to be revealed: ² Be shepherds of God's flock that is under your care, watching over them—not because you must, but because you are willing, as God wants you to be; not pursuing dishonest gain, but eager to serve; ³ not lording it over those entrusted to you, but being examples to the flock. ⁴ And when the Chief Shepherd appears, you will receive the crown of glory that will never fade away.*

You are to be a shepherd but a humble one, who serves and does not seek his own gain. You should be more like Jesus washing his own disciples feet than those who argued about who was greater — Paul or Apollos? This is not about individual reputation but the glory of God.

So, let's move to spiritual fathers. Spiritual fathering is not perfect fathering—it's fathering from a spiritual perspective with eternity in mind. As a Spiritual father, you will need to adapt your parenting to the uniqueness of each child (while still retaining your authority and values). A spiritual father does not overstep the role of the natural father. In fact, if a natural father is present, spiritual fathers work hand in hand in the development of sons, respecting the role the biological father has. The smartest biological fathers I have interacted with have welcome spiritual fathers to add value to their own fathering. Your spiritual father is more like Paul was to Timothy. You can hear Paul's emotion in his words "my dearly loved son."

A pastor may be by your side during key points in your life. But a parent embraces you in his arms each day.

A pastor may encourage you and remind you of God's Word. Your parent cries with you in the midst of things.

Your pastor proclaims God's Word. Your parent teaches and corrects you day in and day out throughout your life.

Your pastor may want to keep you in his pews as long as possible. Your spiritual parent's goal is to make you into a mature adult who can stand on their own. A spiritual parent imparts more than just information into your life they impart themselves into your life.

We will dive deeper into the role of a spiritual parent throughout the rest of this book. So, hold on tight and be in prayer as God's Spirit speaks with your spirit about the roles you are called to.

Chapter 3

Who's The Seeker?

To start with, let me remind you how Elijah started fathering Elisha, as previously addressed in Chapter 1.

And Jehu the son of Nimshi shalt thou anoint to be king over Israel: and Elisha the son of Shaphat of Abel-meholah shalt thou anoint to be prophet in thy room. So he departed thence, and found Elisha the son of Shaphat, who was plowing with twelve yoke of oxen before him, and he with the twelfth: and Elijah passed by him, and cast his mantle upon him. And he left the oxen, and ran after Elijah, and said, Let me, I pray thee, kiss my father and my mother, and then I will follow thee. And he said unto him, Go back again: for what have I done to thee? And he returned back from him, and took a yoke of oxen, and slew them, and boiled their flesh with the instruments of the oxen, and gave unto the people, and they did eat. Then he arose, and went after Elijah, and ministered unto him.

(1 Kings 19)

Elijah and Elisha are probably the greatest example of spiritual fatherhood in the Old Testament. In 1 Kings 19:16, God commanded the prophet Elijah to anoint Elisha to be a prophet. When Elijah found Elisha, he cast his mantle over Elisha. Between that time, and 2 Kings 2, when Elijah was taken up to heaven, Elisha stayed with Elijah and served him. He then received the "double portion" of Elijah's spirit to become prophet after Elijah. These two men represented different generations and opposite personalities, but they were able to walk together.

I want you to see a couple of things from this text to emphasize some different things than what we covered in Chapter 1.

1. Make sure God is involved in selecting your spiritual father.

You should never select spiritual parents based upon their socioeconomical status, because they have a big name or a big church, or because they are your local pastor. Those are the things our society would choose. And our secular culture is far from glorifying God in anything.

Remember, God also choose the unlikely people. They may not be the richest or most handsome or even the most gifted of speakers or the most friendly. However, the Bible is filled with stories of unlikely people God uses in extraordinary ways. Here are some examples.

- The disciples were unlearned fishermen. But Jesus said that to be the greatest in the kingdom of heaven, you should have faith like a little child.
- Isaac, Jacob, and Joseph were all younger siblings. The blessing and greatest inheritance should have gone through the oldest. But Jesus said that the first shall be last, and the last shall be first.
- Gideon was the least member of the least family of the least tribe of all of Israel. But Gideon had faith at least that of a grain of mustard seed.
- Deborah was a woman leader in a patriarchal culture.
- Moses was a murderer.
- Samuel was a man of God who anointed kings, but had trouble raising his own children to be men of God.
- David was an adulterer and murdered to cover up his sin.

But God is the same God today as who used the boy David to defeat lions and Goliath. God spoke to Samuel as a young boy and used him to lead Israel. Moses led the people out of the promised land. God defeated great enemies through Gideon and Deborah. God used the sibling rivalry and deceit of the patriarchs to draw them closer to Him and become great examples of faith. Jesus' disciples changed the world through their faithfulness to tell the good news.

God must be involved in the selection process, or you will experience pain, frustration, possibly a mutilation of your flesh, and spiritual stagnation. Many apostles, pastors, evangelists, prophets, prophetesses, ministers, and teachers have skipped this step and selected the wrong spiritual parents.

The next step in the text that is overlooked or hasn't been taught to the body of Christ is:

2. Spiritual sons and daughters are supposed to pursue spiritual parents, not the other way around.

Shucks, look at the text. Elisha kissed his biological parents goodbye in order to pursue his spiritual father, Elijah. There was no second guessing who was leaving and pursuing whom.

Sometimes pastors, apostles, and bishops are so anxious and braggadocious, trying to make a name for themselves instead of waiting for God to make their name great. So, they start pursing spiritual sons and daughters. While sitting around the clergy round table, partaking of some good soul food, fried chicken, collard greens with smoke ham hocks, cabbage with smoked bacon, hot water cornbread, macaroni and cheese, oak tails, small grain rice (sticky rice), sweet tea, and then for dessert a slice of pound cake and Blue Bell Ice Cream, they began to talk about who they are *over* instead of who they are *under*.

This is *out of order* based upon the aforementioned text. I have seen many people walk hurt because they were pursed by wannabe spiritual parents, instead of the other way round. Spiritual sons and daughters are supposed to pursue spiritual parents. Lord, have mercy on us all!

The verse says that Elisha then left his oxen and ran after Elijah. He said,

> *"Let me kiss my father and mother goodbye, and then I will come with you."*
>
> *"Go back," Elijah replied. "What have I done to you?"*

Notice another thing that this verse tell us.

3. Whenever a spiritual son or daughter begins to pursue the spiritual father, the first thing a spiritual father should do is test the spiritual son or daughter.

The best plan: try to get rid of them! Elijah told Elisha to "go back." Elijah wanted to see how bad Elisha wanted to pursue him.

Many who want to be spiritual parents, or seek it in their own power, would have accepted the spiritual son and daughter immediately, without hesitation. This is why so many people switch spiritual parents as often as they change their underwear.

> *So Elisha left him and went back. He took his yoke of oxen and slaughtered them. He burned the plowing equipment to cook the meat and gave it to the people, and they ate. Then he set out to follow Elijah and became his servant.*

This passage of Scripture ends by saying that Elisha "went after Elijah, and ministered unto (or served) him." Elisha received his training for the ministry by walking with Elijah, serving him, watching him, speaking with him, and ministering with him.

We don't see another thing mentioned in Scripture about Elisha until the day when Elijah is taken up to heaven. This is also the point in time where the prophecy, which God gave to Elijah about Elisha taking his place, comes to pass. As Elijah is taken to heaven, the ministry of Elisha is birthed.

On that day, Elijah and Elisha were traveling together. Three different times, Elijah said to Elisha, "Stay here" because Elijah was going on to another place (2 Kings 2:2,4,6).

All three times, Elisha responded by saying, "As the LORD liveth, and as thy soul liveth, I will not leave thee" (2 Kings 2:2,4,6).

In one way, we can take this as a test for Elisha. Had he not remained faithful to Elijah till the end, he probably would not have received the "double portion" of Elijah's anointing.

Looking back over this passage, let's think about what Elisha did to prove his commitment to follow Elijah.

Elisha was willing to leave what he was doing to fulfill this call. He left what he was doing much like we see the disciples respond to Jesus' call.

He was willing to leave his natural parents to follow Elijah his spiritual father. Although his blood ties to them were strong, Elisha considered God's calling upon him to be even greater. Hello Somebody!

He was willing to make personal sacrifices before stepping into this new call. Once you slaughter the oxen that you were using to plow the fields, there is no going back to that old life. This act signified that there was no turning back, no back up plan if this didn't work out for Elisha.

4. He adopts a servant's role in the relationship with Elijah, even though Elijah had already cast his mantle on him. There was no hint of entitlement, as plagues many people in our culture today. Elisha lived in humility.

5. Elijah created within Elisha the capacity for a double portion of his anointing through the journey they traveled through together.

Even the four places that Elijah had mentioned symbolized the journey Elisha needed to travel on personally, to get to the place where he was ready for this double anointing.

This was not a buddy tour for Elijah to build a few lasting memories to be remembered by. They weren't checking things off Elijah's bucket list. In fact, this was not about Elijah at all. Instead, Elijah the spiritual father, pointed Elisha to God the Father through the reminders of the times God powerfully acted on behalf of His people — Israel.

Gilgal was the place where God and the people of Israel came face-to-face when they finally entered the promised land that God had promised their ancestors Abraham, Isaac, and Jacob long ago.

Gilgal was a place of *renewal* of the covenant. The people took there the physical sign of the covenant in circumcision.

Gilgal was a place of *remembering*. They celebrated the Passover there — their first one ever in the promised land. They remembered somberly how God had delivered them out of slavery in Egypt, so they could enter this land.

But Gilgal was also a place of enjoying God's *inheritance*. They ate of the fruit of the promised land — the land flowing with milk and honey. God had provided in a new way. The old way — manna — stopped the day after they celebrated this meal.

A journey to Gilgal would have served as a reminder of God's faithfulness, teaching Elisha that God keeps His promises.

Bethel was a place that Jacob met God as he was fleeing Esau. God made His presence known to Jacob in this powerful way. God was not limited to any one place. God could be there with Jacob even as he fled. Jacob built an altar there and worshiped God.

Bethel was a place that Elisha would have been reminded of God's covenant being restored with individuals despite the fact that they are sinners. Jacob tricked his father to get the blessing from Isaac. But God made this covenant with Jacob. Jacob had to struggle to get to that place where he could trust — literally wrestling with God.

Bethel was a place that Elisha would have also been reminded that God was with Jacob on the run from Esau, just as he was with the people he brought through the wilderness and into the promised land. God is the God of the in between times, the times of war, as well as the times of peace and safety.

God is not bound by locations or time to help those whose hearts are completely his.

Jericho: After Gilgal, Joshua and the Israelites went to Jericho. On the way, Joshua met the commander of the LORD's army just before the launch of the amazing miracle of Jericho.

Jericho would have taught Elisha that God does the fighting for us when there are impossible odds. That was a powerful symbol for Joshua to obey what God asked him to do — because if you know the commander of the Lord's army is there, His troops are nearby! You better believe that inspired Joshua to obey — no matter how ridiculous it would sound to a military strategist.

Shucks, can you imagine? "I have a great plan to attack this amazing walled fortified city. We need to walk around it silently for 7 days, then shout and blow our trumpets." No military strategist in history would ever plan that strategy. If you had suggested it, they would have laughed. Or worse, you might be out of a job and locked up for lunacy.

But God did plan this very thing – and He delivered! All Joshua had to do was believe and obey.

I imagine this reminder inspired Elisha later when he was surrounded with his servant by an army of human troops. No wonder Elisha knew that God's unseen army was surrounding them. God had delivered Jericho the same way!

Jordan: Again, intertwining the nation of Israel's story with Elisha's, this is where the people crossed into the Promised Land. The priests carried the ark of the covenant into the river, and it stopped. The people crossed on dry land.

As Elijah was taken to heaven and his mantle fell on Elijah, it would have reminded Elisha that God is the same yesterday, today, and forever. He can part the waters of the Red Sea of the Jordan as all of Israel crossed, and as he crossed to the other side.

God too would powerfully be with him as God's mouthpiece to Israel.

God is still at work today. Be prayerful about who you should be taking with you as a spiritual son or spiritual daughter. But remember, this is about Him, not you. You are passing along faith in God, so that your spiritual son can be used by God in a powerful way to impact a new generation for God.

Chapter 4

More than Filling out Forms and Giving Financial Support

A spiritual father's relationship is not forced but grows naturally. Therefore, Spiritual Sons and Spiritual Daughters can connect by their own choice, not because of force or obligation. You cannot develop true spiritual fathering through having people fill out forms or joining an organization. The foundation must be built on adding value in relationship.

There is a major difference between having a spiritual father who provides biblical covering than just being affiliated with a religious organization or doctrinal affiliation. I believe that religious organizations can give you papers to fill out and a front row seat at the annual conference, but they can't give you empowerment or close up experiences, and they can't unlock the dormant gifting and that only spiritual fathers are mantled to release.

This process takes place via covenant relationships through spiritual fathering (as God does everything via covenant). By covenant relationship I simply mean that the Holy Spirit establishes the relationship, and we recognize that we have a covenant with God in that relationship and that we honor the relationship as such. From a biblical perspective one's covering should be their spiritual father. Joseph told his brothers that God had made him a father to Pharaoh; [8] *"So then, it was not you who sent me here, but God. He made me father to Pharaoh, lord of his entire household and ruler of all Egypt"*. (Genesis 45:8 New International Version)

Elisha cried 'my father, my father' when Elijah was taken into heaven; Paul was Timothy's spiritual father, etc). In other words, teachers are common and abundant in our lives, but fathers are rare and exclusive who provide us with covering and not just filling out forms.

> *"I have received full payment and have more than enough. I am amply supplied, now that I have received from Epaphroditus the gifts you sent. They are a fragrant offering, an acceptable sacrifice, pleasing to God"*.
>
> (Philippians 4:18)

It is clear as you read Paul's epistles. He had some dedicated and serving followers and friends. You can read more than once about Epaphroditus, Timothy, and

Luke. They were the ones with Paul in the worst of times. It is clear the people of Philippi gave to Paul out of the overflow of thankfulness they had for him as a spiritual leader in their lives. They gave out of thankfulness and not obligation.

Paul, again and again, wrote to thank these who helped him and shared the gospel message no matter the harsh circumstances they faced. These followers were willing to give up their safety and security — even possibly their lives — to share together with Paul in the face of sharing in Christ's sufferings.

We have a clear picture of how Baranabas shepherded Paul, how Paul and Barnabas both shepherded the people at Antioch, and how Paul shepherded Timothy. Their lives and purpose in sharing the gospel were intertwined.

Today's culture is something completely different. Maybe it is because of prosperity in America. Maybe it's a generational thing, and the younger generations today think they are entitled to everything that previous generations earned. However, we do have institutionalized processes in our churches and seminaries to help train the next generation of pastors.

The credentialing and endorsement process is crucial in creating a healthy context for ministry. This process makes the covenant pastor (spiritual son or daughter) accountable to their spiritual father, whom they have discerned to lead them, as well as to the community of pastors in the Covenant Ministerium.

Some spiritual sons and daughters only want to connect

with a spiritual father for credentials and the ability to name drop without any submission to their authority. They are seeking spiritual fathers in name and status only — not with the training, teaching, and discipline that spiritual fathers offer.

These sons and daughters do not have continual communication with their spiritual parents. They don't honor them consistently. They don't show up to annual leadership impartation or even do so long distance. They believe as long as they fill out a form and send in a few dollars as an obliged thank-you offering that they are in right standing with their spiritual father.

They are not transparent with leadership and always have an excuse why they don't clear their calendar to sit at the feet of their spiritual parent's leadership at the annual leadership impartation. Many are not transparent about their church financials. They are neither transparent about their 501(c)3 status, or lack thereof, nor their marriage.

The relationship has a *form* of godliness only. There is not spiritual depth. There is not obedience. There is not servanthood and submission. They do not understand that you must submit to spiritual fathers *first* and then have them fill out the form.

Shucks, you don't argue. You don't defend your issues. You don't put your rights and ideas first.

You submit. You learn. You sit at the feet of your spiritual father. If you ask questions, make sure they are for clarification — not opposition. This is not a time for me-first thinking.

Hello somebody!

This has been one of the most neglected dimensions in the church. Actually, God knew that it would be, so He declared that He would set out to have this dimension fully restored in the end-times.

> *"Behold I will send you Elijah the Prophet before the coming of the great and dreadful day of the Lord. And he will turn the hearts of the fathers to the children, and the hearts of the children to their fathers, lest I come and smite the earth with a curse."*
>
> *(Malachi 4:5-6.)*

This Scripture can be applied both at the level of the natural family and in the church. As we look around the earth today, we can see so many children being raised in a single or non-parent environment. This, in many instances, is the continuation of a vicious cycle that has left many without proper fathering.

We see this trend in the land of opportunity — America itself — so know that things are even more difficult across the globe. I pray for a new generation of men who face up to their responsibility, admit their mistakes, make a relationship with their children, and lead the next generation to know God and follow Him.

This area of fathering has also been neglected in the church, and we have seen the same devastating effect — and sometimes greater — as many have been raised without proper fathering.

A spiritual father is more than just a "godparent." A spiritual father is someone who cares for us, who imparts love, identity, and spiritual covering to us. A spiritual father prays for us and is concerned for our well-being. Dare I say, a spiritual parent is on hands and knees before God, praying for us.

I see Abraham praying over Lot and begging God to spare the righteous in Sodom. I see Isaac praying for the rift between Jacob and Esau that he helped cause through favoritism. I see Joseph telling his brothers that what they had planned for evil, God had been able to use for good and salvation. I see Moses begging for the people of Israel as they complained before God. I see Jesus mourning over Jerusalem, longing to take them under his wings as a mother would to her children. Our spiritual parents love us in this way, intercede for us, and ask God to act on our behalf and draw us closer to Him.

In return, we love, honor, serve, and care for our spiritual father. We also give, in return, to make our spiritual father's work easier. We are partners in ministry but more specifically co-laborers. We are concerned about the work and letting God reap the profit.

God puts people in our lives to bless us, lead us, and spiritually parent us. However, we have to let them in. A spiritual father is someone God has placed in our lives for our spiritual well-being. We should submit to them, give our hearts to them, and serve and honor them. In return, God will bring good to us through them. They are a source of life to us through Christ.

> *"Be on alert, stand firm in the faith, act like men, be strong."*
>
> *(1 Corinthians 16:13 NASB.)*

Paul's message to the Corinthians was a strong one. In fact, we know there is a missing letter that had been referenced which was particularly harsh on them. That may be why a copy was not saved of this letter — we literally don't have an existing copy that we can see today.

But Paul makes it clear to them, that the Corinthians are to be strong and take responsibility for abandoning sin and following God. They need to work as a unified body. They need to be spiritually mature, move past the milk fit for infants, and feast on the full gospel and theology of Christ.

We can make excuses for our behavior. Maybe it is because we were raised in a single parent home. Maybe we don't know our biological father. Maybe we have been mistreated by police, bullied by gangs, attacked by users, and ignored by people who called themselves Christians, but lived as hypocrites.

But God calls you to make a choice to follow Him. It is clear in the Old Testament Law. Sin has its consequences. Sin does impact the children to the third and fourth generation. We are impacted by the sins of our fathers.

BUT you *can* break that cycle. You can be the one who changes your family tree. God might allow sin to impact a family tree for a few generations, but for those who follow Him, God promises to bless their offspring for 1,000 generations! Shucks, I will take that deal.

I think that's why as Joshua aged, he was determined to remind people of how God was faithful to them. But, he drew a line in the sand. He did not mince any words. He told the people, "Choose today who you will serve."

Today is a day of decision. Today is what matters. Don't put it off to tomorrow. Don't delay. Today is the day of salvation.

Joshua responded on behalf of all of his family: "As for me and my household, we will follow the Lord."

And the people were convicted. I imagine they were not only convicted by the Holy Spirit, but the weight of the faithfulness and obedience of Joshua throughout his life. This is the same Joshua who God had to tell three times in Joshua 1 to "be strong and courageous." After all, they were getting ready to enter the promised land and were going to face armies of strangers.

But Joshua responded. After hearing from God he went to the people and said that they were moving out in three days. I don't know about you, but I think that is pretty strong and courageous. Three days until I enter a land that I know will be filled with conflict.

I admit too often I am skilled at avoiding conflict. Joshua was not. Joshua did not hesitate to follow God's directions into Jericho either.

That was the encouragement and bravery with which Paul urged others to be strong and act like men. You and God together make a majority. With God, you are more than a conqueror. Take action! With God leading the way, you can't fail.

Spiritual children, trust your spiritual father to lead you

based on his years of experience trusting God through the good and bad times.

Spiritual fathers, continue to pour your life and work into your spiritual children. Be a powerful example as Joshua and Paul were to those they shepherded. Before I exit this chapter, let me share something that is often overlooked.

Always remember that a famine exists when the heavens over your ministry are shut down, and if you want to have them open over your ministry here is how you do it. Honoring the tithe covenant through your 'spiritual father/covering'. Yes, tithe up to your covering church. This will open the heavens over your life and release an untold number of destiny resources that you need to succeed. Many pastors challenge their members to tithe and this is awesome, but I believe that your church should also tithe up to the covering ministry of your spiritual father.

Consider that the model in the Word is that even the priests were commanded to 'tithe up' to the high priest that was over them. Numbers 18:26-28 (Easy-to-Read Version)[26] "Speak to the Levites and tell them: The Israelites will give one-tenth of everything they own to the Lord. That one-tenth will belong to the Levites. But you must give one-tenth of that to the Lord as your offering. [27] That tenth will be your offering to the Lord. It will be like grain from your own threshing floor or wine from your own winepress. [28]

In this way you will also give an offering to the Lord just as the other Israelites do. You will get the one-tenth that the Israelites give to the Lord, and then you will give one-tenth of that to Aaron the priest. Connecting with your spiritual father and spiritual mother as the Holy Spirit has appointed to your life and then honoring the tithe principle is a major key to God breaking famine - financial famine, relational famine (personal isolation and disconnectedness), circumstantial famine, and revelational famine out of your life. Many people, regardless of age, long for spiritual fathers and mothers. If that's you, I want you to ask yourself: am I willing? Are you willing for spiritual parents to speak into your life, to bring discipline and correction? You've got to choose to be present as often as possible, to open up your life to them. In a church context, that starts with showing up to a midweek Bible study and, as you get to know them more, invite them to speak into your life. Share what's going on with you, and pursue relationship with your spiritual parents. God's Word for God's people!

Chapter 5

Spiritual Abuse Versus Spiritual Correction

Hey, hold on wait a minute, take a deep breath, and relax. I'm not saying that spiritual abuse isn't possible and has never happened to anyone before. I do understand that there are some horrible, selfish, mean-spirited, manipulative spiritual parents out there. As a pastor and spiritual father, my heart is broken over situations like that.

But, I haven't seen spiritual abuse much at all. I've seen bad stuff. Tough stuff. Inconvenient stuff. Emotionally difficult stuff. Unfair stuff. My heart goes out to those who have been treated poorly by spiritual parents, but you don't correct wrong teaching by not teaching at all.

You correct wrong teaching by right teaching, and that's

my goal in this chapter.

Likewise, my heart goes out to spiritual parents who have been treated poorly by spiritual sons and daughters, who misinterpreted correction for abuse. Incorrect expectations of spiritual parents can easily lead to offense. As part of the church, too many presume it's the spiritual parent's responsibility to *always* coddle them and to jump through their hoops 24/7. Child, please, that's not biblical at all.

What I'm saying is that there is a difference between spiritual abuse and spiritual correction. It's a sad commentary that for years, and even today, many so-called spiritual sons and daughters have been, and are currently being, outsmarted by the enemy and divorcing spiritual parents by the thousands and hindering their own spiritual development. I have witnessed many today who are leaving churches by the droves because of the most ridiculous reasons. When they don't get what they want, they accuse the spiritual parent of control or spiritual abuse of authority.

> *[11] The point is that we shouldn't be outsmarted by the Satan. We know what he's up to!*
> *(2 Corinthians 2:11 New Testament for Everyone)*

Sorry, folks, but correction is not spiritual abuse. Discipline is a part of life. We may not realize it, but without discipline, we accomplish nothing. Throughout our lives, we either need to discipline ourselves, or we need to be disciplined by others.

In the early years of our lives, that discipline is imposed upon us by others, specifically by our parents. Babies and young children do not have any capacity for self-discipline, so they need help in that area. Without discipline, they will constantly find themselves in danger, without even recognizing the danger that they're in. The type of discipline they need is to teach them about those dangers and how to avoid them.

But, being disciplined by others teaches them how to discipline themselves. Gradually, children learn what is dangerous and what they should avoid. Some of those lessons are learned from their parents as they learn to obey, and others are learned by not obeying their parents and suffering the consequences. Ouch! That stove's hot! Shucks!

Unsurprisingly, little ones don't like being disciplined, but they need it none the less. The same can be said of us as we grow older. A college student who doesn't study for his exam gets a bad grade from the professor. The student calls it "unfair." Yet, is it fair for that student to get a good grade without working for it? If they were disciplined and did what they should, they probably would have gotten that good grade they wanted.

Everyone balks at discipline. This is universal, from the smallest child to the greatest of men. Actually, that small child may have an easier time accepting discipline than the man does, because as a child, he is more accustomed to receiving it. At some point along the way, though — probably in our teen years, when we are sure we know everything — we decide that we no longer need to have others discipline us.

Yet without discipline, growth stops. Discipline is a necessary part of growth, driving us to make the effort necessary to seek out what we lack and then to overcome it.

This is easily seen when we look at people working out at the gym. Some work out diligently, pushing their bodies to the limit on a regular basis. This soon becomes obvious, as their muscles grow. Others, who don't push as hard and aren't as regular are just as obvious, as we can tell by their lack of growth.

The same can be said for just about any area of human growth. More importantly, it can be said for our spiritual growth as well. Spiritual growth isn't something that comes to us automatically. It only comes through the application of discipline to our lives. Either we learn how to apply that discipline ourselves or we need someone to help us by taking the place of our spiritual father or spiritual mother and disciplining us. Well, spiritual parenting works the same way. Our spiritual fathers correct us for our own good. They actually have a mandate from God, because they are our spiritual fathers, to correct us when we need it. In love, yes, but still to correct. They would be horrible spiritual parents if they did not.

Over my years in ministry, I get nauseated every time I hear rebellious, stiff-necked spiritual children pull the "spiritual abuse" card whenever they get corrected, and ready to disconnect from their spiritual parents just because they do not want to be told when they are wrong, out of order, and told to sit down in ministry until further notice. Trust me, I know correction is discomforting sometimes.

I've been corrected by my spiritual mother and father before and, still even to this day. Hello, somebody!

I will tell you right now that it is not always enjoyable. I do not enjoy it, not even one bit. But I need it, and God in His mercy has allowed me to be spiritually corrected and not abused. He has placed my spiritual parents in my life who give me valuable feedback which is helping me grow in life and ministry. I don't want to disappoint my spiritual father and mother. I don't want to sin against God, and I don't like the embarrassment of needing to be corrected.

But if I do — God help me — I pray He'd correct me, because I know He gives more grace. And I'd rather be kept on the straight and narrow path (even if it hurts), than wander into rebellion or sin.

Brother, sister, correction is for our own good. And God has placed our leaders over us because, well, *we need them*. Romans 13:1 tells us that God Himself has placed us under the leadership of our authority figures.

So, what exactly is spiritually disciplining? What does it look like?

Our greatest example of this comes from the Lord Himself and His relationship with His disciples. The 12 men He selected as His first and closest disciples were men who walked with Him, and worked with Him, as Jesus went about His ministry here on Earth. Knowing that He would not be able to continue teaching and healing in his physical form forever, He selected these men, that

He might be able to reproduce Himself in them. That required making changes to their beliefs and understanding, as well as working on their character. To do that, He had to discipline them.

Jesus essentially put his disciples through a three year spiritual boot camp. His goal, just like a drill sergeant, was to remake them into new men; turning them from carnal men to spiritual ones. That required a considerable amount of discipline and correction along the way.

We don't normally think of it as such, but Jesus constantly disciplined His disciples. Fortunately for us, they wrote those experiences down in the gospels, so that we might learn from them. There are many examples, like the many times he chastised them for their lack of faith.

> *Now when He got into the boat, His disciples followed Him. ²⁴ And suddenly a great tempest arose on the sea, so that the boat was covered with the waves. But He was asleep. ²⁵ Then His disciples came to Him and awoke Him, saying, "Lord, save us! We are perishing!" ²⁶ But He said to them, "<u>Why are you fearful, O you of little faith</u>?" Then He arose and rebuked the winds and the sea, and there was a great calm.*
>
> (Matthew 8:22-26)

When we read this same story in Mark, Jesus said to them *"Let us cross to the other side"* (Mk 4:35). Since Jesus had said that, there was enough power in those words to get them across to the other side, storm or no storm. Yet, when the disciples saw the wind and waves, their faith faltered and they woke Him, crying out in fear.

Jesus didn't chastise them for not knowing how to save themselves; He chastised them for their fear and their lack of faith. He knew that His disciples would have to face much more serious dangers in the future, without Him being there in bodily form, to take care of it for them. If they operated in fear, instead of faith, they would perish. So He chastised them, disciplining them as part of teaching them how to move in faith, rather than fear.

Over and over again, we see Jesus chastising His disciples, those who were closest to Him, for their lack of faith. I'm not talking about the "name it and claim it" type of faith here; but rather the type of faith they needed to have in order to do His work.

In chapter 17 of Matthew's gospel, a man brought his son to Jesus' disciples so that they might cast a demon out of him. This was while Jesus was on the Mount of Transfiguration. It's pertinent to note that Jesus had already given His disciples authority to cast out demons in Matthew 10:1, a long time before this event. It's safe to say, they had probably done so on numerous occasions. Yet they couldn't do it this time. So the man brought his son to Jesus, who cast the demon out (Matt 17:15-18).

We know this story mostly through the words of Jesus, where He said that *"this type of demon only comes out by prayer and fasting."* But before Jesus said that, He once again rebuked His disciples, in private, for their lack of faith:

Then the disciples came to Jesus privately and said,

> *"Why could we not cast it out?"* [20] *So Jesus said to them, "<u>Because of your unbelief</u>; for assuredly, I say to you, if you have faith as a mustard seed, you will say to this mounting, 'Move from here to there,' and it will move; and nothing will be impossible for you."*
>
> (Matthew 17:19-20)

There was no cruelty in Jesus' words or actions. He wasn't punishing them for what they had done. Rather, He was pointing out to them where they were at fault, specifically, in still harboring unbelief. His chastisement had the purpose of teaching and correcting, not of making them look bad in front of others or even feel bad for their failure.

There's a huge difference between correction and punishment. While both may take the same or similar forms, the difference is in the purpose. Whenever we are the ones to administer the correction, we must be sure that our hearts are right, so that we don't slip over into punishment.

Perhaps it's easier to understand the difference when we talk about a child who has done wrong. Many parents use corporal punishment, spanking their child for those actions. But what is their purpose? Some might be spanking with the thought "You do the crime, you do the time." That's pure punishment, the idea of making someone pay for what they have done wrong.

But there is no real place for punishment in the Body of Christ. Jesus has already borne the price of all our sins on the cross.

> *Who Himself bore our sins in His own body on the tree, that we, having died to sins, might live for righteousness – by whose stripes you were healed.*
>
> (1 Peter 2:24)

This verse makes clear that we don't have to be punished for our wrong actions; our sins. Therefore, it follows through that our children don't have to be punished for their sins, for Jesus bore those on the cross, just as He did our own.

Yet the verse goes farther, saying that we have died to sins and therefore might live for righteousness. Herein we find the other reason a parent might spank their child; to instruct them in righteousness. This is correction, discipline, instruction and chastisement; but it's not punishment. There is nothing in the heart of the parent, saying that they must make that child suffer for what they've done. Rather, there is love for the child and a desire to help them grow into a godly adult.

The same thing can apply to a spiritual father correcting his spiritual son. The key becomes, what's the motive? What godly characteristic is the spiritual father trying to instill in his son's mind and heart? What does he want to teach his son?

In the examples from Jesus' life and ministry I showed you above, it was all about teaching his spiritual sons (disciples) to walk in faith. There is nothing in what Jesus said or did that can be seen as punishment of any sort. If anything, He went out of his way to make sure that the chastisement was done in private, just Him and the disciples, so that they wouldn't even be embarrassed.

Any sort of discipline applied without love, is prone to turn into punishment. That's an important key. If we are going to provide true discipline, rather than punishment, we must express love for the one receiving the punishment throughout the process. It's not enough that we feel that love in our hearts, the recipient needs to feel it as well.

Let me return to correcting a child once again. Parents who only spank their child when they've done wrong haven't demonstrated love to them, even though they might have felt that love in their heart. Telling that child, "This is going to hurt me, more than it hurts you" isn't going to work either. A much more tangible expression of love, which the child can feel, is needed.

That's why it's so important to take the time to talk to that child, before spanking them, explaining what they are being corrected for and turning it into a teaching moment. Then, equally important, the parent needs to hold that child, while they are crying afterwards, until they stop crying. Finally, the parent needs to reaffirm their love for that child, assuring them of their love for that child.

While spiritually disciplining a spiritual son doesn't actually include spanking them, it does still require taking the time to explain what the spiritual son did wrong, as well as to express love to them, so that they know that they are still loved, regardless of the mistake made.

If we go back to Matthew 17, where the disciples couldn't cast out the demon, we find that Jesus didn't just use that situation to talk about their unbelief, but also to teach them. He said, *"for assuredly, I say to you, if you have faith as a mustard seed, you will say to this mountain, 'Move from here to there,' and it will move; and nothing will be impossible for you."* (Matt 17:20). That was something He had never understood before, taking their understanding of faith up another notch.

Jesus didn't stop there though. He had taken advantage of the teaching moment, but perhaps his disciples were still feeling bad. So he needed to do something about that. He did, saying, *"However, this kind does not go out except by prayer and fasting"* (Matt 17:21) letting them off the hook in a way, by essentially telling them *"It's okay that you failed. This was a lesson you hadn't learned yet."*

Of course, we know that this wasn't an isolated demonstration of Jesus' love for His disciples. There were countless others. While He was trying to rebuild the spiritual sons He had chosen into the spiritual giants we know them as, He was constantly affirming them, letting them know that they were special to Him. There could have been no doubt in any of their minds that Jesus wanted them as part of His inner circle, specially chosen by Him.

We don't have any trouble with being told we're special and that we're loved; but that's about the only part of what Jesus did which we don't have trouble with. There are many people today who are unwilling to accept any sort of teaching, let alone correction or instruction. They rail against it as if it were some sort of abuse.

But true discipline or correction, given in love, isn't abusive whatsoever. So where did this idea that it is abusive come from?

Sadly, this idea comes from the world we live in. Today's society tells people that things aren't their fault. Any problem in their life, whether it is something they don't do right or some result that doesn't turn out right, can't possibly be their fault. It has to be someone else's. They are merely a victim of what those unnamed others have done to them.

But isn't this attitude antithetical to Christianity? Isn't our salvation based upon our acceptance that we are sinners and Christ died to pay the price for that sin? We aren't sinners because of what others have done to us, but rather because of what we ourselves have done wrong. Therefore, if it were not for Jesus' sacrifice on the cross, we would need some means of paying the price for that sin ourselves. It is through His and the Father's love for us, that we are spared paying that price.

Repentance for our sins is an integral part of the salvation experience. What is someone receiving forgiveness from, if they don't recognize their sins and doesn't turn away from them?

While our salvation makes us *"a new creation"* (2 Cor 5:17), where *"old things have passed away and all things have become new,"* the old man doesn't like that. That old man isn't as wont to just get up and leave as he should be. He literally has to be driven out. How? Through discipline.

When a spiritual father corrects his son, he is helping that son to drive out the old man. Rising up and complaining about the father's actions just helps to prove the necessity for them hello somebody. Any son who is complaining about their father's discipline without first taking a good look at their own heart, to see where the father is right, is denying that the father is their father. At the same time, they are denying themselves the benefit of that relationship.

So, what should we do, when faced by spiritual correction?

The first step is to stop and listen ... truly listen. Don't try to defend ourselves or explain away our actions. Just try to make sure that we understood what was said. Even if there was good reason for what we did, and even if we can justify our actions, that's not the point. The point is to learn the lesson that our spiritual father is trying to teach us. If there is any need to explain our actions, it is secondary; coming after learning.

Ask questions to clarify your understanding. There's an awful lot of misunderstanding in the world today, even (or perhaps most especially) between people who know each other well. There's no way of learning the lessons that need to be learned, without understanding.

Once the basic understanding is there, it's time to go deeper, discussing the issue and how to apply it to your life. If your spiritual father is trying to teach you something, you want to make sure that you get everything you can out of it. Don't assume; ask and learn. Discuss and understand. Get the whole of the lesson, so that you can put it into practice in your life.

Once you've done that, always leave the meeting on a positive basis. You never want to walk away feeling hurt or discouraged. This relationship is important to you;

maintaining it is more important than any one particular lesson.

Does spiritual abuse exist? Yes, it does; although much of what's labeled "spiritual abuse" is anything but. So how can we tell if something is spiritual abuse? What defines it as such?

There might be several different definitions for this, but Jesus gave us a pretty good idea in Matthew's gospel:

> *"Be wary of false preachers who smile a lot, dripping with practiced sincerity. Chances are they are out to rip you off some way or other. Don't be impressed with charisma; look for character. Who preachers are is the main thing, not what they say. A genuine leader will never exploit your emotions or your pocketbook. These diseased trees with their bad apples are going to be chopped down and burned.*
>
> *(Matthew 7:15-20 The Message)*

Just who are these wolves? How do we know when they come? What do they do?

Fortunately, Jesus told us that too, "Don't be impressed with charisma; look for character." In other words, wolves come amongst the sheep because they are hungry; they want to eat the sheep. So the real question is, is the person who you think is abusing you trying to feed you or feed off of you? Shucks Pastor Bryant, preach on preach on!

We've all seen this; the traveling minister who comes to "minister" to the church, but puts more effort into trying to get the congregation to buy their books or support their ministry. They're not feeding the church; they're feeding off of the church.

But if they're not trying to feed off of you, they're not wolves. Nor are they abusing you. Oh, they might not be coming across the right way; they might even be missing the mark in how they're trying to minister to you. But they're not abusing you. Whatever they're doing, even if it is not done the best way possible, is done out of love and done for your benefit.

Keep in mind that your spiritual father is trying to bring about some positive results in your life; things which are for your benefit. It shouldn't be surprising if he or she does or says some things you aren't going to like. We all struggle against change, and the more closely held a particular idea, belief, action or sin are, the more we struggle against letting it go. But the more we struggle, the more letting that thing go is going to hurt.

We must believe that our spiritual father is being led by the Holy Spirit in what they do. Otherwise, why did we select them to be our father? So with that in mind, when we struggle against what they are trying to do, we are also struggling against the Holy Spirit Himself; we're struggling against God.

What seems like abuse is probably the very thing we need. Yes, it might hurt; growth often dose. If you don't believe me, ask the guys with the big muscles in the gym. They'll tell you, "no pain; no gain." That little phase doesn't just apply to lifting weights, it literally applies to every area of human growth that you or I can find. Physical growth hurts, intellectual growth hurts, and spiritual growth hurts as well.

The life of a believer is supposed to be one of continuous growth. Salvation may be the work of an instant but sanctification is the work of a lifetime. It is a work that we begin on the day we become saved and we should still be working on it the day that we die. None of us have arrived at sanctification yet, we are all still in that process.

But, to become sanctified we need first to know what is wrong in our lives. God has two basic ways of showing that to us:

- The first is His Word, which speaks to us and acts as a mirror of our souls.
- The second is sending us someone to speak a word of correction into our lives, such as the prophets did.

Obviously, it's much better to be corrected by the first rather than the second of those. Our Heavenly Father is a God of love, who will always treat us with love. His servants are the same. They may not love as perfectly as He does but they still act from love, especially when they are acting in His holy name.

So faint not when you are corrected, but rather rejoice in that correction. It is proof that you are one of God's sons, rather than some illegitimate child that somehow snuck into the crib. For God chastens those He loves, and one of the ways He does that is though His servants.

> *⁵ And have you forgotten his encouraging words spoken to you as his children? He said, "My child, don't underestimate the value of the discipline and training of the Lord God, or get depressed when he has to correct you.⁶ For the Lord's training of your life is the evidence of his faithful love. And when he draws you to himself, it proves you are his delightful child." ⁷ Fully embrace God's correction as part of your training, for he is doing what any loving father does for his children. For who has ever heard of a child who never had to be corrected? ⁸ We all should welcome God's discipline as the validation of authentic sonship. For if we have never once endured his correction it only proves we are strangers and not sons.*
>
> *(Hebrews 12:5-8 (The Passion Translation)*

Yes, it hurts when we are corrected. That's normal. Correction is not fun. It's not pleasant. But it is necessary. We all need it. Not only does it prove that we are sons, rather than illegitimate children, but it ultimately helps us to become more like our Heavenly Father. And isn't that what the Christian life is supposed to be about?

There will never come a time in our lives when we don't need correction. Just accept that as fact. We don't reach a point of perfection, where God no longer needs to correct us; it just doesn't happen. And since we don't always hear what His Word is saying to us, He sends people to us who will help us get the message; the spiritual fathers He has placed over us.

I know it's hard, but learn to accept correction with joy. Then and only then, will you get the maximum benefit out of it. Besides, if we're going to be continually corrected until we die, we may as well learn how to receive it with joy. Otherwise, we'll be miserable all the time.

Can it be accepted with joy? Of course it can. We see example after example of people in both the Old and New Testaments who were corrected either by Jesus Christ or by Jehovah God. Some fought against that correction and others accepted it with joy, but they all received it. How much better to do it as David did, when Nathan the prophet went to him, exposing his sin?

In 2 Samuel, chapter 12, Nathan the prophet sternly rebuked King David for the sins of sleeping with Bathsheba and then arranging for her husband, Uriah the Hittite, to be killed in battle when it turned out that she was pregnant. Nathan could only have known this because of the Holy Spirit revealing it to him. It would have been easy for David to deny it, calling Nathan out as a false prophet. But he didn't; in repentance he said:

> *"I have sinned against the Lord." And Nathan said to David, "The Lord also has put away your sin; you shall not die."*
>
> *(2 Samuel 12:13)*

How much better for David, that he accepted that rebuke, even being king, and was restored. Had he not, it would have ultimately cost him much more. Rather than just having his pride temporarily bruised, he might have lost his kingdom and his life.

Would calling Nathan's words spiritual abuse have been worth it, at that price? Was his pride so important, being king, that he should have refused what the prophet said? No; and neither should we. Whether our spiritual fathers are prophets or not, we should accept them as such in our lives, taking their words as coming from the throne of God and applying them to our lives as quickly and thoroughly as we can.

I beseech you by the mercy of God for you to embrace the spiritual correction God has sent your way, believing that He knows better than you do. Even when it hurts. Spiritual correction is for your own good. It's called "good parenting," and it's essential when we're doing life together as the Body of Christ. It's not spiritual abuse it's spiritual correction. Now walk in love!

Chapter 6

Go Purchase Your Parents a Knife

Not all spiritual fathers are equal. Just as different pastors view their roles uniquely and have a different vision given from God, so too, different spiritual fathers see their roles differently. Some view their role organizationally, as if they were running a company, where they were "in charge" of their spiritual sons. But this institutional format defies the example that Jesus demonstrated to us. He didn't start the "Jesus Christ Evangelistic Association." He called men to follow Him as disciples, learning not only from His teaching, but also from their relationship with Him.

True spiritual fatherhood is about relationship, not organization. One can learn knowledge and skills from an organization, but one cannot have their character molded and shaped by it. Yet, true biblical training is about forming character, not checking off boxes on a form.

The book of Proverbs tells us:

> *He who spares his rod hates his son, But he who loves him disciplines him promptly.*
>
> *(Proverbs 13:24)*

Why does that father discipline his son? It's not just to show his love, and it's certainly not to punish him. It's to make positive, necessary changes in the character of the son. It's instructive, not in the academic way, but in a much deeper way, driving foolishness from him and instilling wisdom in its place.

> *Foolishness is bound in the heart of a child. The rod of correction will drive it far him.*
>
> *(Proverbs 22:15)*

We are accustomed to applying these verses to raising children, but isn't that what a spiritual father is doing? Isn't he raising spiritual sons to fulfill their place in the Kingdom of God, doing the Lord's business?

The word *disciple* refers to one who is following a leader and is "under discipline" from that leader. That doesn't mean punishment, but rather training to adhere to rules or a code of behavior. What rules and code? Those described to us throughout the Bible.

When Jesus chose his disciples, He wasn't looking for

men who were ready for ministry. Nor was he looking for Talmudic scholars. He was looking for men who he could mold and form, training their character, as He trained their minds and hearts. He was looking for men who He could turn into copies of Himself.

> *For him He foreknew, He also predestined to be conformed to the image of His Son, that He might be the firstborn among many brethren.*
> *(Romans 8:29)*

Through the years of His ministry, Jesus traveled with his disciples. He talked with them, ate with them, cared for them, taught them and rebuked them. None of that was written down in a curriculum or guide, it was teaching and training in the moment, using each experience they encountered as a learning moment, as another opportunity to make them a little more like Himself.

This sort of relationship is sadly missing in much of the church today, even in the ministry. We spend a couple of hours Sunday morning and maybe Thursday night listening to the pastor. In that time, he is supposed to counter all the influence of the world, helping us to grow into that image of Christ. But where is the part where the pastor is given an opportunity to work on our character? Other than in counseling sessions, he or she has very little opportunity to do so.

When our young men and women feel the call of God on their lives, we send them to Bible schools, where they sit in class and fill their heads with knowledge. But where is the part about forming godly character in them? Unless their parents had already done that part, most are sadly lacking. Yet we are supposedly preparing them for the work of showing others how to follow Jesus and conform their hearts and lives to Him.

Had Jesus used a modern Bible school to train His disciples, Christianity would not have survived. It's not that I have anything against Bible schools, but because they are lacking in character preparation, they are spitting out people who are unready for the calling they are supposedly preparing to fulfill. Just look at these statistics:

- Fifteen hundred pastors leave the ministry each month due to moral failure, spiritual burnout, or contention in their churches.

- Fifty percent of pastors' marriages will end in divorce.

- Eighty percent of pastors and eighty-four percent of their spouses feel unqualified and discouraged in their role as pastors.

- Fifty percent of pastors are so discouraged that they would leave the ministry if they could, but have no other way of making a living.

- Eighty percent of seminary and Bible school graduates who enter the ministry will leave the ministry within the first five years. Ninety percent of pastors said their seminary or Bible school training did only a fair to poor job preparing them for ministry.

- Ninety percent said the ministry was completely different than what they thought it would be before they entered the ministry.

- Seventy percent felt God called them to pastoral ministry before their ministry began, but after three years of ministry, only fifty percent still felt called.

- Seventy percent of pastors constantly fight depression.

Where is the lack that is causing these horrendous statistics? One strong possibility is the lack of a relation with a true spiritual father. Many ministers feel like they are "spiritual bastards," although they can't really articulate the feeling. The problem? They need a father.

The Apostle Paul wasn't Timothy's natural father. Nor was he the father of Titus. Yet he "adopted" these two young men as spiritual sons. Their personalities were quite different, but their calling was the same, to preach the gospel and pastor the sheep.

We don't know how much time Timothy and Titus spent seated at Paul's feet, traveling with him and learning from him; we only know that they did. This was very much a part of Paul's ministry and why we have his letters in the New Testament.

When we read about Paul's ministry in the book of Acts, we can see that the Holy Spirit of God directed him to city after city, where he gained a following of disciples, trained them up, founded a church (not a building, but a congregation), prepared leaders, and left those leaders in charge of that congregation, as he went on to other cities to do the same thing over again.

Yet Paul never broke ties with any of those churches he founded. Rather, he kept in communication with them through his writings. The Pauline Epistles in the New Testament are Paul's ongoing effort to continue discipling those ministers, his spiritual sons, and the flocks under their care.

We really don't know how many letters Paul wrote. He could have written hundreds. All we know is what we have. But there are places where those letters do make reference to others which we don't have. For example, in the book of First Corinthians, Paul writes:

> *I wrote to you in my first letter…*
> *(1 Corinthians 5:9)*

What first letter? Does that mean that our First Corinthians is actually Second Corinthians and we're missing the first? Then he writes in what we call Second Corinthians 2:3-4, referring to his "sorrowful letter." But this doesn't seem to fit the tone of our First Corinthians. Is he referring to the missing first letter, or is there a third letter which came between the two we have?

There is also a reference to a letter he wrote to the Laodicean church, telling the Colossians to share the letter he sent to them with the church there, and that they should likewise read the letter that Paul had sent to Laodicea. We find that reference in Colossians 4:16, yet that epistle doesn't exist today.

Paul's ministry was accomplished fully through relationships. He didn't have a website or radio program. He wasn't on TV. There was no YouTube. He ministered person to person or through his letters. Even then, his letters were a personal expression of his love for those pastors and their churches, individually crafted to meet their particular needs and deal with the specific struggles they were having in those churches.

Yet of all Paul's spiritual sons, however many there were, Timothy appears to have had a special relationship with him. Paul encountered him in a town called Lystra and wanted this apparently remarkable young man to travel along with him in the ministry.

> *Then he (Paul) came to Derbe and Lystra. And behold, a certain disciple was there, named Timothy, the son of a certain Jewish woman who believed, but his father was Greek. ² He was well spoken of by the brethren who were at Lystra and Iconium. ³ And Paul wanted to have him go on with him. And he took him and circumcised him because of the Jews who were in that region, for they all knew that his father was Greek.*
>
> *(Acts 16:1-3)*

We don't know how Timothy came to be saved, but we

know it was not through Paul. We read in these verses that he was already a disciple when Paul came to know him. Not only that, but he was well regarded by the brethren, not only in his own town, but in the neighboring town of Iconium. There's no specific reference to say why he was known, but it could have been though some service he offered to the believers or that he was already ministering to them in some way. Whatever it was, this young man impressed Paul to the point that Paul wanted him working and training with him as a spiritual son.

There was just one little problem. Timothy's father was a Greek, and the Jews knew it. So Paul circumcised his new spiritual son, Timothy, according to God's covenant with Abraham (Genesis 17:10-13).

But was that all there was to it? Was it merely a form of subterfuge or camouflage, so that the Jews would accept Timothy amongst them? If that was it, then it was falsely done. Since we know that Paul was a Pharisee by training (Acts 22:2-5; Phil 3:5), it would be against all his training and his nature to perform a circumcision under such false pretenses. There had to be something more in Paul's mind.

God established circumcision with Abram, when he returned to reaffirm His covenant with him, changing his name from Abram to Abraham. It was a sign of that covenant, not something done merely as an ID badge of the Jews. Nobody walked around showing of that ID badge. Paul, following in Moses' footsteps, was bringing Timothy into that covenant, so that he would better be able to serve God and fulfill God's will for his life.

Paul's personal spiritual fathering role is seen most clearly in his relationship with Timothy. Paul, heeding the advice of the brethren, selected Timothy to travel with his ministry team (Acts 16:2).

Timothy came from a family in which his mother was a believer, and his father was not (Acts 16:1). Timothy had a strong Christian heritage from his mother, Eunice, and his grandmother, Lois (2 Timothy 1:5). Yet Timothy needed a spiritual father in order to reach his full potential in Christ. Paul called Timothy his son (1 Timothy 1:2, 18; 2 Timothy 1:2; 2:1) in the faith. The model of Paul and Timothy is one of the clearest in Scripture for defining the roles of spiritual parents and spiritual children.

The writings recorded in 1 and 2 Timothy are instructions of a spiritual father to his spiritual son, and Timothy's faithful discharge of service is a prime example of the commitment needed by spiritual sons and daughters. Timothy served Paul in the good times and the bad (Acts 16). Timothy could be trusted (Philippians 2:19–20). Timothy was empowered by Paul to do the work of ministry (1 Timothy) and was corrected by Paul in the midst of that work (2 Timothy). At the end of his journey, Paul's spiritual son, Timothy, ministered to the aged apostle (2 Timothy 4:9–21).

This was something the Jewish people took seriously and still take seriously today. One who is not circumcised is not part of that covenant. In fact, God said:

> *And the uncircumcised male child, who is not circumcised in the flesh of his foreskin, that person*

> *shall be cut off from his people; he has broken My commandment.*
>
> *(Genesis 17:14)*

This is such a serious issue with God, that God had to deal with Moses directly about it. When he and his wife, Zipporah, were traveling to Egypt, after the 40 years on the other side of the desert, the son of Moses became ill, nearly to death. This was clearly understood by both parents to be because of their disobedience in not following God's command to Abraham and circumcising their son. So Zipporah circumcised her son, thereby saving the life of their son.

In a similar manner, God commanded Joshua to circumcise the men of Israel, just after they crossed the Jordan River into the Promised Land. That whole generation had grown up in the wilderness, born to parents who had lived their lives in Egypt. We don't know when, but somewhere during all those years, they stopped circumcising their sons, so that whole generation was uncircumcised:

> *At that time the Lord said to Joshua, "Make flint knives for yourself, and circumcise the sons of Israel again the second time."*
>
> *(Joshua 5:2)*

God takes His covenants seriously, and since circumcision was a covenant act, He took that seriously as well. But if that is so, then why doesn't He require circumcision of us today? Should all Christian males be circumcised?

There are several verses in the New Testament which talk of this, giving us insight into what Paul was doing in his circumcision of Timothy:

> *For no one is a Jew who is merely one outwardly, nor is circumcision outward and physical. But a Jew is one inwardly, and circumcision is a matter of the heart, by the Spirit, not by the letter. His praise is not from man but form God.*
> *(Romans 2:28-29)*

> *For we are the circumcision, who worship by the Spirit of God and glory in Christ Jesus and put no confidence in the flesh.*
> *(Philippians 3:3)*

> *In Him also you were circumcised with a circumcision made without hands, by putting off the body of the flesh, by the circumcision of Christ.*
> *(Colossians 2:11)*

God still requires circumcision, but like many other things in the New Testament, He is more concerned about a circumcision of the heart, rather than a circumcision of the flesh. You and I are circumcised, when we give our hearts to Jesus and worship God alone.

Paul circumcised Timothy as an outward sign of an ongoing inward act; one in which his heart was circumcised by God Himself. It was a necessary act for a number of things to happen, in order to bring Timothy into the next phase of his life and ministry.

- Circumcision clearly established his personal covenant with God the Father, through the blood of Jesus Christ. While he inherited the right to the Abrahamic covenant by right of birth, through his mother, the Christian covenant is not inherited. Even though his mother was in covenant with God, as a believer in Jesus Christ, Timothy could not inherit that. He had to establish his own personal covenant with God, just as we do when we are saved.

- He gained credibility with the Jews that he would be ministering to. While he did not need physical circumcision to be saved, it made him more acceptable to the Jews.

- When Paul circumcised Timothy it wasn't because he was participating in something evil, but he cut off things that will hinder his effectiveness for the Kingdom of God. He cut on private places and sensitivity areas, which is a metaphor for us to let us know that spiritual leaders need to speak into in pride and private areas of our life in order to expanded our ministries so that people can receive our ministry gift. Remember the people knew Timothy's father was a Greek (non-believer) "Paul came to Derbe and then to Lystra, where a disciple named Timothy lived, whose mother was Jewish and a believer but whose father was a Greek" Acts 16:1. Therefore people while not want to receive from him so his spiritual father circumcised in or to expanded his spiritual sons influence.

- Since Paul was the one to circumcise him, it established covenant between the two of them as well. Being in covenant together established their father-son relationship, giving Timothy the right and ability to receive all that Paul had for him.

- By allowing himself to be cut in the flesh, Timothy symbolically cut himself off from the things of the flesh, so that he could focus on the things of the spirit. This is not to say that he was turned into a eunuch, but that he was putting the things of the spirit in a higher place in his life, as compared to the things of the flesh.

One thing about circumcision; it can't be taken back. Once someone is circumcised, they're circumcised for life. Oh, I suppose that some plastic surgeon could come up with a way to make a new foreskin, but why? Could that undo the circumcision of the heart? Could it undo the work that God has done?

We don't know if Paul told Timothy he wanted to circumcise him, or Timothy brought it up to Paul. It really doesn't matter in their case, as we see the results. But that doesn't mean that it doesn't matter in our case. Since circumcision is a sign of the covenant, it's an important part of any spiritual father-son relationship.

Am I suggesting a physical circumcision? No. I'm talking about a spiritual one. More than that, I'm talking about the spiritual son coming to the spiritual father, wanting to come into covenant with him. A spiritual son asking to come into covenant with his spiritual father is much more than one who is just looking for someone to take him in.

We are no longer a covenant society, but the people of the Old Testament were. Today, we've replaced covenants with contracts, and everyone knows the saying that "All contracts are meant to be broken." That's not the same as covenants though; they are a permanent commitment, something that lasts down through the generations. In fact, God refers to them lasting up to 1,000 generations.

Covenants are often referred to as "blood covenants," hence, the need for a knife. While God commanded that they circumcise the male foreskin, most cultures that utilized covenants cut the hand or arm of the two who were joining into covenant and mixed their blood. Later, something would be put into the wound, ensuring a visible scar as a testimony of their covenant. The American Indians were a covenant people, practicing this and becoming "blood brothers," while the European settlers had no idea what a covenant was.

Whenever someone in covenant would meet others, they would raise their hand in salute. This showed the other party their scars, letting them know, "If you mess with me, you're messing with my covenant brother too." It was reported that the explorer Stanley, famed for the line

"Dr. Livingstone, I presume" had cut covenant with over 50 tribal chieftains, with all those scars visible on his arm. I doubt anyone would want to mess with him.

Why was that important? Because when two people are in covenant, they'll do anything for each other. If you and I are in covenant and someone tries to kill you, I have a moral obligation to not only protect you, but to go after them, killing them if they have harmed you.

But it goes farther than that. If you come to me in need, I must give you whatever I can, even if it is to my own harm. This isn't an "Oh, I have to" sort of giving grudgingly. It's giving with joy. It's meeting you at the door, welcoming you, and asking what I can do to serve you. It's a desire to give, for no other reason than because you are my covenant brother. Of course, that goes both ways, so both end up receiving the blessing.

It's not hard to give to someone you're in covenant with, because the attitude is, "What's mine is yours, and what's yours is mine." It's the sort of attitude we're supposed to have when we get married. That's actually not surprising, since God created marriage as a covenant too.

There's a word that's central to covenant. That's the Hebrew word *"haced."* It's the word that we understand to mean God's unconditional love, translated in the Old Testament as either lovingkindness or mercy. It's also the kind of love that people in covenant have towards each other, totally unselfish, totally giving. Most of us know it better by the Greek word *"agape."* But that is actually only a Greek translation of the Hebrew word.

After Jesus was raised from the dead, he asked Peter if

he loved him, using the word *agape*. But Peter was only able to respond that he had *fileo* love for Jesus, a brotherly love. He hadn't reached that point of truly loving Jesus as he should (John 21:15-17).

In responding in this way, Peter was admitting that he wasn't at that point of covenant love. He was there for what he could get out of his relationship with Jesus, not fully understanding that he had to give as well. He would grow to that point, but he hadn't reached it yet.

Buying your spiritual father a knife, even if it is only symbolically, is committing to being in covenant with him. That's important if you want to receive all you can from him. Without that level of commitment, you're merely a fair-weather follower, there for what you can get out of the relationship. But once you truly enter into covenant, that means you're committed to the relationship, as long as you are both alive.

This obviously isn't something to be entered into lightly. If you can't handle criticism and correction, you don't want to be in a covenant relationship with a spiritual father. But, if you're not willing to accept that correction, and you haven't fully accepted him as your father; you're just playing games.

We all need correction in our lives. That's part and parcel of the life of a believer. God is constantly working in us, to bring about change, bringing us to a place of godliness. He uses those who are in our lives, especially those who are in a position of authority, to help bring about that change. But what would happen if we chose to walk away from a spiritual father, rather than accepting the correction he offered us?

Walking away is walking away from our own spiritual growth. Yet every week, literally thousands of people walk away from their church, because they were offended by something the pastor said or preached. In other words, the pastor touched on something they needed to change in their lives, and they didn't like it. Rather than face their problem and change their life, they chose to say bad things about their pastor and walk away.

This person obviously isn't a son and can hardly be called a true church member. But sadly, it's not uncommon at all. There are way too many people filling our churches, who are only there to get into heaven, without wanting the things that God wants in their lives here in this life.

Correction is part of the deal. It's not just about knowing someone famous, influential, or powerful. Just as a natural father corrects his children, accepting someone as a spiritual father is agreeing to accept his correction too; otherwise, he's not really your father.

This is why it's up to the son to symbolically buy his father a knife. Doing so sends a message. It shows his commitment. It shows that the son is willing to put something into the relationship too, not just taking something out of it. And yes, I'm talking about actually buying your spiritual father a knife. It's a nice manly gift, which will always be appreciated.

How good a knife you buy is up to you, but that will send a message too. Cheap knives aren't all that great. Besides looking cheap, they don't work all that well, and the blades dull quickly. A good knife, on the other hand, will not only be beautiful, but functional, lasting a long time. As with any other good quality gift, it can send the message that the recipient is important to you.

What do you get in exchange for that gift? You get the same things that Timothy got from Paul, by allowing Paul to circumcise him. It won't help you as far as credibility with the Jews, but it will help you with your relationship with your spiritual father.

Remember when Jesus said, "Where your treasure is, there your heart will be also?" It's found in Matthew 6:21 and Luke 12:34. It's often misquoted as "Where your treasure is, there your heart is also." But it reads as "will be" and not "is" in both verses. In other words, your heart follows your treasure. So when you invest in something, either by making an offering to the church or giving a gift to someone, your heart will follow your actions. You will become more closely connected to him, loving him more.

In this case, your gift will make you more connected to your spiritual father. You will feel closer to him, making it easier to receive that correction when it comes. But it will also make it easier for you to receive everything else he has for you. The more you invest in that relationship, the more you will receive.

Chapter 7

I Have Been Mutilated

Men and women who have suffered verbal or physical abuse at the hands of their biological fathers incline to mistrust spiritual fathers and authority.

I believe that our brains are trained to make associations with either pain or pleasure based on our upbringing. An abused son or daughter will associate all father figures with pain and abuse. Consequently, they will tend to shy away from spiritual fathering until they are healed of their past so they can trust again.

Also, some women and men have experienced pain in the church when so-called spiritual fathers have used them for their own recompenses and abused or abandoned them. If this transpires in someone's first experience with a spiritual father, they will tend to mistrust all future spiritual fathering, even if they come across a leader with the right heart and motive toward them. Also, when a woman or man experiences a perceived rejection from a spiritual father figure it is hard for them to start all over and trust another spiritual father figure, even if the rejection was only perceived and not real. Since many women and men would rather handle pain in silence than face the pain of rejection, they never allow themselves to enter into that type of relationship again with another spiritual father.

God has always used natural things to teach spiritual truths. That's why Jesus used so many parables in His teachings. This concept isn't limited to just Jesus' parables though. There are many other examples in scripture, such as Paul using marriage as an example of our relationship with Christ in Ephesians 5:32.

Why is this so? Why does God choose to teach this way?

He is using what's familiar to us. As natural beings, we receive information about the world around us through our natural senses. We experience life in his natural world and are intimately familiar with it. So when God speaks to us about spiritual things which we are not familiar with, He uses those natural examples that we already understand. Those natural examples are supposed to show us spiritual truths.

Of course, these analogies only go so far, as we are no longer the agrarian society that existed in the time of Christ. So we don't have as clear an image of caring for sheep or planting seed that they did back then. Even so, we can still connect to some extent with these daily activities, because they happened here in this physical world we inhabit. We've all seen enough examples to at least have a basic understanding of them, even if we haven't done them ourselves.

But then there are things we all understand ... or at least all of us should understand; like the relationship between a husband and wife or a father and a son. The problem is, the society we live in has changed even that; imposing non-traditional ideas on gender roles and norms, just as they have on marriage. This affects our understanding of spiritual truth as well, especially when scripture uses that natural relationship as a means to teach us spiritual principles.

One of the ways this has happened is in the increase of single-parent homes. A woman can't teach a man how to be a man, no matter how hard she tries. Only a man can do that. Neither can a woman teach a man to be a father. We learn fatherhood by watching our own fathers practice it. Good or bad, we learn from their example, how they father us.

A man who fathers a child, but didn't have a good example of fatherhood from his own life, struggles to be a good dad. Most fail miserably at it.

Likewise, a man who doesn't have the example of growing up (spiritually) under a good spiritual father doesn't really know what it takes to be the father his sons need. Without the direct intervention of the Holy Spirit, teaching him, his is unlikely to be an effective spiritual father. Even with the direct intervention of the Holy Spirit, he is unable to fulfill that calling, unless he fully submits to the leading of the Spirit.

Another thing which has changed with time, is our understanding of covenant ... or perhaps I should say our lack of understanding of it. What used to be a common way of forming agreements has been replaced by contracts, mere paper agreements, which don't carry the same level of commitment that covenants did. Breaking a contract is no big deal, while breaking a covenant would very likely result in death in many parts of the world.

Our God is a God of covenant. Everything He does is through covenant relationship. We see many examples of Him making covenant with people in the Old Testament, such as His covenant with Noah after the flood (Gen 9:11) and His covenant with Abram (Gen 15). He even refers to His Son as the mediator of a New Covenant:

> *For this reason Christ is the mediator of a new covenant, that those who are called may receive the promised eternal inheritance – now that He has died as a ransom to set them free from the sins committed under the first covenant.*
>
> *(Hebrews 9:15)*

This new covenant built upon the old, improving upon it. It is also ratified in a better blood, as it was created in the blood of Jesus Himself (Matt 26:28), not that of bulls and goats. But, make no mistake of it, God has not done away with covenants altogether. He hasn't even done away with the old covenant.

In other words, He hasn't changed, nor has the understanding of covenant changed. We have. And we have because the society we live in is no longer a covenant society. As such, there's a risk that we won't take our relationship with God, as our covenant partner, as seriously as we should.

There are a couple of important concepts which are central to covenant. Understanding them helps us understand our relationship with the Lord, as well as any other covenant relationship we enter into, such as marriage and having a relationship with a spiritual father.

The first and most important of these is the concept of love — not romantic love or even fraternal love, but unconditional love, God's kind of love. The love that is meant by the Greek word *agape*. That kind of love can't waver with the tides of a relationship. If anything, it becomes stronger when the chips are down. It is a love that loves not because of who the person is, but in spite of it. When two people come into covenant, they have committed to having this kind of love from then on, no matter what.

When we have that sort of love, we give preference to the other person (Rom 12:10), rather than expecting it for ourselves. It is a giving sort of love, which is concerned about the well-being, needs, and even desires of the other.

That love causes the concept of "remembrance," such as when the people of Israel were groaning in their captivity and God "remembered" His covenant with Abraham (Ex 2:24). We tend to take that word as meaning that something had been forgotten and then remembered, like the guy driving home from work who suddenly remembers that his wife had called, asking him to pick up milk. But when the Bible uses that word in relation to God, it's more like, "He had them at the forefront of His mind." He hadn't forgotten; He was thinking of them all along.

Another concept that comes out of that love is how they handle property. Covenant requires the attitude that, "What's mine is yours, and what's yours is mine." So, when we remember our covenant partner has needs, we are quick to give, with joy, even if that means giving our last dollar.

Finally, that love gives us the concept of permanence in the relationship. You don't just end a covenant because of a misunderstanding or a disagreement. Rather, you realize that it is your responsibility to find a way to overcome the problem and maintain the relationship, till death do you part.

When two people enter into covenant, there is a cutting and mingling of blood. That's an essential part of the covenant ceremony. It is a symbolic act, with the significance that "My blood now flows through your veins, and your blood now flows through mine. We are now one."

It's also done to create an unforgettable memory. You don't just forget blood. Oh, you might forget about a paper cut or something else that's minor, but you can't forget about something serious. There's something about the sight of blood, which burns a permanent memory into our minds, one that is easily recalled.

Since our God is a God of covenant, we would expect this to be a part of our relationship with Him, and it is. In Genesis 13, God made circumcision a commandment for Abraham and his descendants, long before the law was given to Moses.

> *This is my covenant with you and your descendants after you, the covenant you are to keep: Every male among you shall be circumcised. ¹¹ You are to undergo circumcision, and it will be the sign of the covenant between me and you. ¹² For the generations to come, every male among you who is eight days old must be circumcised, including those born in your household or bought with money from a foreigner - those who are not your offspring.*
>
> *(Genesis 17:10-12)*

It is interesting that God chose this particular place for the men of Israel to have to cut themselves and bleed, as a sign of the covenant. Normally, in other covenants, cuts were in the hand or forearm, so that when they raised their hand in greeting, it would show that they were in covenant. But God purposely chose a place where it would not be shown, while at the same time being in a place where the men could not forget that their flesh had been cut because of that covenant. They would be reminded of their covenant on a daily basis.

But you might ask, where was the part where God's flesh was cut as part of the covenant? That happened a couple of thousand years later, at the cross of Calvary. Since God lives outside of time, the two co-existed. That's really not an issue for Him, although it can cause some confusion for us.

Today, whether or not a baby boy is circumcised is considered a medical decision that's made in the hospital, when the child is born. Some doctors recommend it, and others don't. But most Christians don't consider it much of an issue to be concerned about. Nor, does it seem, that God is really all that concerned about it, because His bigger concern is whether or not we are circumcised in the heart, not whether we are circumcised in the flesh.

> *The Lord your God will circumcise your hearts and the hearts of your descendants, so that you may love Him with all your heart and with all your soul, and live.*
>
> *(Deuteronomy 30:6)*

> *No, a man is a Jew (worshipper of Jehovah God) if he is one inwardly: and circumcision is circumcision of the heart, by the Spirit, not by the written code. Such a man's praise is not from men, but from God.*
>
> *(Romans 2:29)*

God has never turned His back on His covenant with us, nor will He. That would be totally against His character. Rather, He will uphold those covenants to 1,000 generations.

> *Know therefore that the Lord your God is God; He is the faithful God, keeping his covenant of love to a thousand generations of those who love Him and keep His commands.*

(Deuteronomy 7:9)

Just for comparison's sake, we've only come about 400 generations from Adam, so it will be a long time yet to come before God comes to the end of the first covenant He made with mankind, let alone the last. He will remain faithful much longer than any of us will be here on this Earth.

In today's western society, circumcision is done by the doctor who delivers the baby. But in the Jewish culture, there is an official in the synagogue who performs ceremonial circumcision, which is called a *Birt Milah*. This official is called a *Mohel* and has been trained in performing the ritual.

The idea of being circumcised by someone who is not properly trained in the ritual is a bit scary, even though Moses' wife, Zipporah, did it to their son, using a flint knife nonetheless. But what about the circumcision of the heart? Can that be mishandled by someone who doesn't know what they are doing? It most certainly can.

We read earlier that the circumcision of the heart is accomplished by God, more specifically by His Holy Spirit. So how can I say that it can be mishandled? Because the person who brings us to that point may not do so correctly, which would result in a great misunderstanding of this circumcision.

As human parents, there are two important covenant relationships we bring our children into. The first of these is with ourselves. The responsibility of being a parent is that of a covenant with that child, even if the child may not fully reciprocate in kind. The second is with the Lord. This is the single most important thing we do with our children, ensuring that they have a relationship with Him.

But how do we do that? Some parents try to get their children into a relationship with the Lord by taking them to church, expecting the preacher to get them saved. But that may not work. The best possible way any parent has of getting their child to fall in love with the Lord is to live that way before them. Children may not do what their parents say, but they will follow their parents' example.

Those same two covenants exist in the spirit, just as they do in the natural family. A spiritual father must hold his relationship with his sons as a covenant relationship, as well as drawing them further and further into a covenant relationship with our Heavenly Father.

But what about a spiritual father, who doesn't have those relationships himself? That's dangerous. While a good teacher will always strive to help their students surpass themselves, the truth is that it's very hard to do that. Most of us need a good example, so that we will know how to love the Lord with all our hearts, as well as understand the father/son relationship we are in.

Someone being in the ministry is no guarantee that they have a deep intimate relationship with Christ. It may not even be a guarantee that they are saved, although finding an unsaved person who is in the ministry is rather rare.

Even so, there are a lot of people in the ministry who have lost their first love and are merely going through the motions. They're still caring for the sheep, still counseling, still preaching, and still running the church or ministry that the Lord entrusted to them. They're just not doing it with the passion and love for God that they started out with. As such, they are unable to pass that same love on to others. Spiritual children of these fathers are unlikely to end up having a passionate relationship with the Lord.

In this case, it would be really challenging to find a way to say that the spiritual father is fulfilling the role they've been called to fulfill. They weren't fulfilling the first requirement of good spiritual parenting, giving their spiritual child a love relationship with Christ.

While it is possible that the spiritual son might overcome the failings of their father in this case. The lukewarm relationship that the spiritual father has with the Lord will make that harder. It's more like the father will be getting in the way of the son's relationship with the Lord, then the father will be accomplishing anything to encourage it.

I wouldn't want to be in that spiritual father's place, when it comes time to give account before the judgment seat of Christ.

But there's something that might even be more serious than this, that's the spiritual father who mutilates their son, trying to circumcise them. Without knowledge in how to properly circumcise, there is great risk that the spiritual father will cause more harm than good, mutilating them.

How can one possibly understand how to circumcise another, if they have never been circumcised themselves? How can one teach another how to be a good spiritual son, if they haven't been one either?

King David was called by God to be king over Israel, after King Saul failed. It shouldn't be any surprise that Saul failed, as he never truly had a relationship with the Lord. When Samuel remonstrated with him for not obeying God and bringing back the best of the animals from his attack on the Philistines, Saul tried to get out of it by blaming the men for bringing back the best of the animals to sacrifice to "the Lord your God" (1 Sam 15:15). Why didn't he say, "the Lord my God?" Apparently because he didn't feel that the Lord was his God, only Samuel's.

Yet this is the same king that David served in the palace, after being anointed to become king. In the first part of 1 Samuel 16, Samuel goes to the house of Jesse, the father of David, and anoints him as king. Then in the second half of the chapter, David was brought into the palace to play music for the king, because he was being tormented by an evil spirit.

How could David learn to fulfill his calling in such an environment? Saul, who should have served as his spiritual father, was incapable of doing so, because he himself was not circumcised in heart. He had no relationship with God, so he could not show David how to have one. Fortunately for David, he had his own relationship and didn't need to rely on learning from King Saul.

But there's more to this story. David was not only skilled with the harp, but he was the one to kill Goliath (1 Sam 17). He was a great warrior in battle, so much so, that the women sang,

> *Saul has slain his thousands, and David his ten thousands.*
>
> *(1 Samuel 18:7)*

This of course enraged Saul with jealousy, who decided to take matters into his own hands.

> *The next day an evil spirit from God came forceful upon Saul. He was prophesying in his house, while David was playing the harp, as he usually did. Saul had a spear in his hand* [11] *and hurled it, saying to himself, "I'll pin David to the wall." But David eluded him twice.*
>
> *(1 Samuel 18:10-11)*

This was the first time that Saul tried to kill David, but there were others. He could never get over his jealousy or fear of David, perhaps even discerning in some way that God had called David to succeed him as king.

Later in the same chapter, it tells us that Saul sent David off to battle the Philistines, thinking,

> *"I will not raise a hand against him. Let the Philistines do that!"*
>
> (1 Sam 18:17)

Then Saul once again tried to pin David to the wall with a spear (19:9-10). After this, David fled, living in the wilderness with men who would have probably been political prisoners, had they not made good their own escape.

Instead, they became David's mightiest warriors.

While Saul was not a godly man or even a spiritual one, we must remember that he was the king of Israel, chosen by God to fulfill that role. Since Israel was God's chosen people, called to serve Jehovah Himself, Saul should have been a spiritual leader. Many have speculated about why he wasn't, but that's not our point right now. As he stood in that role of king, he was a father figure, and, as such, he failed.

Had Saul accepted God the Father as his Father, things probably would have been different. But he didn't. Therefore, he didn't have anything spiritual to give David, only death. And he tried to give that to David several times. Rather than providing the means to a circumcision of his heart, Saul tried to mutilate him. Only the grace of God protected David.

The only interest the Sauls of this world have in anything spiritual is to use it to gain personal power. He did this towards the end of his reign, when he was once again confronted by the Philistines. Samuel had died, so Saul didn't have his counsel (not that he really followed it). But he was going into battle and he wanted a sign. So:

> *He inquired of the Lord, but the Lord did not answer him by dreams or Urim or prophets. ⁷ Saul then said to his attendants, "Find a woman who is a medium so I may go and inquire of her."*
>
> (1 Samuel 28:6-7)

Clearly, Saul didn't have a relationship with God, or he

wouldn't have sought his answer through a medium. Yet he disguised himself and tried to have this woman call up the spirit of Samuel. Whether or not it was actually Samuel who appeared, he looked like Samuel, and he said:

> *Why do you consult me, now that the Lord has turned away from you and become your enemy? 13 The Lord has done what he predicted through me. The Lord has torn the kingdom out of your hands and given it to one of your neighbors – to David.*
>
> *(1 Samuel 28:16-17)*

Here it is, the reason for Saul's hatred of David. Regardless of whether Saul had known it before, here he is told that David will succeed him as king. But by this time, David is out of his reach, living in the town of Ziklag, in the territory of the Philistines.

Saul's spiritual condition made it impossible for him to be the spiritual father David needed. He could not help prepare David to be king, unless it was purely accidentally. Rather, he tried to mutilate David, even to kill him. He was uninterested in what God said, and what God had called David to do. Rather, he was only interested in himself and therefore tried to kill David as a threat to his own comfort.

This story of Saul and David shows us the importance of selecting the right spiritual father. It was impossible for Saul to give anything to David that might benefit him, because he didn't have it himself. Being the first king of Israel (other than God Himself), he didn't have anyone to show him what to do. As a worldly man, he took temporal power, thinking that was enough. He tried to lead from his own power, which wasn't enough. Then, when someone came along who had more personal power and ability, he tried to kill him.

Such things exist in the Body of Christ as well. While we are unlikely to see anyone who claims to be a minister of the Lord grab a spear and throw it at their spiritual sons, it's not at all farfetched to think that they would do the spiritual equivalent, trying to use their position to cause their children harm and destroy any potential ministry they might have.

Such things have always happened, ever since the beginning of the church. There were supposed ministers who were traveling around, telling Greek believers who received Christ that they needed to be circumcised in the flesh. They too were "mutilators of the flesh" and were called out as such, by none other than Paul himself:

> *Watch out for those dogs, those men who do evil, those mutilators of the flesh. ³ For it is we who are the circumcision, we who worship by the Spirit of God, who glory in Christ Jesus, and who put no confidence in the flesh.*
>
> *(Philippians 3:2-3)*

There are many different forms which these people can take today. One is legalism, the establishment of a list of rules, which don't appear in scripture, but are "interpreted from scripture," which bind people up and prevent them from growing in Christ.

But legalism isn't the only way they mutilate the flesh, and legalism itself can actually take many forms. Religion, as a replacement for relationship with the Lord, is another such form. That will mutilate one, just as much as legalism will. In either case, any relationship with the Lord becomes covered up by the form of religion, something that tries to make us holy by imposing something upon our flesh, rather than dealing with the spirit.

This too, is a form of mutilating the flesh, as it is flesh-centered, rather than spirit-centered. The life of a believer and the life of any spiritual son must be spirit-centered in order to be effective.

> *Since, then, you have been raised with Christ, set your hearts on things above, where Christ is seated at the right hand of God. Set your minds on things above, not on earthly things.*
>
> *(Colossians 3:1-2)*

Going back to that passage in Philippians, we can also see how to find those who are not mutilators of the flesh, in that it defines the true circumcision. In other words, it shows us who are those, who are circumcised in the heart, those who *"worship by the Spirit of God, who glory in Christ Jesus, and who put no confidence in the flesh."* When you find someone who meets those requirements, you'll know that you've found someone who is more interested in circumcising your heart, than circumcising your flesh.

In reality, any spiritual father/son relationship needs to

have a worship component to it. Seeing someone worship tells you a lot about their relationship with the Lord. Hearing them talk about it helps us to understand the depth of their love (or lack thereof). Worshipping together is sharing a time of intimacy with the Lord together. This is something that can draw us closer to each other, as we draw closer to Him.

The true circumcision of the heart can only happen in the presence of the Lord, because it is a work of the Holy Spirit, as we've already discussed.

Therefore, finding a spiritual father who will lead you into worship, rather than leading you only into a relationship with themselves, ensures that you will receive what you need from the Trinity: Father, Son, and Holy Spirit.

Chapter 8

Childhood Before Parenthood

I am so tired of seeing so-called spiritual fathers and mothers trying to be spiritual parents to sons and daughters without being spiritual sons or daughters first. Therefore, as it is in the natural world so it is in the spiritual world, too. You cannot become a parent before you first experience life as a son or daughter.

In the natural world, this makes perfect sense. We know that we are born first and grow up as infants, then toddlers, then children, then teenagers, and then young adults. There is a natural order ordained by God through which parents raise their children, teach them, call out their giftedness, and launch them into life as adults. This stage cannot be skipped, though many attempts to father without processing sonship in their own life. This is what separates the true spiritual fathers from the rest. They have learned to walk as a son before their Father in heaven and before true fathering influences here on earth. It always shocks me when people attempt to live as spiritual fathers when they have a track record of refusing any fathering relationship for themselves. Shucks!

You can look around and see that God created things that way. Everything in society is built around this truth. Look at how schools are graded and how eventually you graduate into the next stage. Look at how we even size clothes, shoes, and other products based on age. All assume a progression from younger to more mature.

There is a reason why it is impossible to have children before a certain age biologically. And most would agree that, even if an adolescent is physically capable of having children, they should not until several things happen, such as an education, life experiences, maturing in decision making, and growing in skills and job-related training so that you can support yourself before having a family. There are certain things that are essential in order to launch successfully as a self-supporting adult in our society — not to mention finding a soul mate and entering a covenant marriage relationship.

But many spiritual parents have skipped stages in the spiritual process. After all, we are often taught to be independent as quickly as possible and learn to depend on ourselves. But we all need a spiritual parent there and know how to submit to his authority and leadership. We need a model to show us the way before we start leading someone else down the right path.

The Problem in Today's Church

Let me tell you, the problem in today's church is not that different than it was in Bible times. People tried to do things out of order then as well. Paul sent Timothy to the Corinthians because they did not understand spiritual sonship, and Paul as a spiritual parent. But he and Timothy modeled it perfectly.

Churches today are not run like a family but a business. We focus on numbers and the bottom line more than relationships. We talk about growth and success more like a business does, than the early church that grew daily because they ate together, worshiped, sat under the apostles' teaching, and had everything in common.

> *⁴²They devoted themselves to the apostles' teaching and to fellowship, to the breaking of bread and to prayer. ⁴³ Everyone was filled with awe at the many wonders and signs performed by the apostles. ⁴⁴ All the believers were together and had everything in common. ⁴⁵ They sold property and possessions to give to anyone who had need. ⁴⁶ Every day they continued to meet together in the temple courts. They broke bread in their homes and ate together with glad and sincere hearts, ⁴⁷ praising God and enjoying the favor of all the people. And the Lord added to their number daily those who were being saved.*
>
> *(Acts 2:42-47)*

They did not grow because their spreadsheets and business plans rivaled the best businesses of the day!

Our churches have become democratic bodies either run by the vote of the people or by the church bureaucracy of our denominations. But God's desire is for Jesus to be the head of the church. Things are out of order — backward — and God allows disorder to get our attention. Instead of vibrant, mature leaders taking the lead, things begin to happen out of order.

> *"4. He says, "I will put young boys in charge of you. They will be your leaders. 5. The people will turn against each other. Young people will not respect those who are older. The common people will not respect important leaders."*
>
> (Isaiah 3:4–5)

When the people of God refuse spiritual maturity in Christ Jesus, they are judged by losing maturity and have immature individuals in leadership positions. The fathers were replaced with children. This implies that there is a time when those who are spiritually mature in Christ are replaced with those who lack maturity. If you have not been a spiritual son yourself yet, you cannot be a spiritual father. You lack the maturity to do so! When the Apostle Paul tells the Corinthians that they have, "For though ye have ten thousand instructors". The word for "instructors" here in the original Greek is paidaggos, and it doesn't have anything to do with angels. In modern English we have an corresponding word—"pedagogue," which means a teacher, especially a dogmatic or pedantic one. In Paul's day, paidaggos was the term for slaves whose job it was to take or lead their master's children to and from school. The literal meaning of "paidaggos" is child-leader, and by implication, it meant a tutor, an instructor, or a schoolmaster. The ancient pedagogue was responsible to protect the child from evil influences and associates, and to keep him or her safe from physical and moral harm. He was to see to it that the child arrived at school on time and later to bring him or her safely back home. Today we might call that person a nanny or a baby sitter or a childcare worker. To be sure, all of these duties and responsibilities are also the concerns of a father, but for a babysitter it is only a job and a paycheck on Friday at the end of the week. Shucks, babysitters come and go. I said babysitters come and go. The question becomes do you want a baby sitter or a spiritual father? A child could have 10,000 babysitters while growing up. To make his point Paul said, one could have ten thousand instructors or guardians. In contrast, however, a child has only one father. For that one person, that one father, the care, protection, and nurture of his child are not just his job, but his heartbeat. Paul was referring to his own relationship to the Corinthians so he used the term: "father," because he considered himself to be their spiritual father, not just their instructor or guardian. He doesn't want to put them to shame. He only wants to admonish them, to warn them. He speaks to them like a father, and he wants them to imitate himself. He offers to come to them in a spirit of gentleness. Scolding gives way to tenderness. "I am not writing this to shame you, but to warn you, as my dear children. Even though you have ten thousand guardians in Christ, you do not have many fathers, for in Christ Jesus I became your father through the gospel. Therefore I urge you to imitate me. [verses 14-16]

When Paul says, "imitate me," he isn't being ego-centric or puffed up. No, this is the guy who called himself "the chief of all sinners," and he knows that he is not perfect. This is not arrogance. It represents Paul's very understanding of what it means to be their spiritual father. But you may be saying that you have the best education money can buy and you have a great pastorate. All that may be true, but it can't replace the experience of that close relationship with a spiritual father.

Listen, please stop requiring from spiritual sons and daughters what you haven't first required from yourself. True spiritual parents are people that we do life with — they are with us for the good and bad days. Natural parents change diapers, get up in the night, discipline, and also celebrate their children. In the same way, spiritual parents walk with you through the issues of your heart. In tragedy or triumph, they're there for you and will pray for you.

Think about this in the natural. If your biological parents never changed your diapers or disciplined you, then how would you know how to effectively do that for your biological children?

I submit to you, please first become a spiritual son or daughter. It will allow you to effectively be a spiritual parent to others. It's called law and order. There's a natural order to things.

I don't know about you, but I think there's a natural order to how we expect things to work in our lives. What if you went to a surgeon for surgery and he told you that he had never gone to medical school and submitted to learned doctors to train him? He explained to you that he had learned everything he needed to know from YouTube videos. I don't know about you, but I'd be walking out the door as soon as possible!

You would never dream of becoming an instructor to fly a plane if you never had flown yourself. That's ridiculous! Spiritual parents should have the same kind of shock at the thought of trying to lead someone else in anything you have never experienced yourself.

Those who do things out of order don't have a strong sense of identity. They will be blown by the wind more often than those who are grounded by a parent's relationship. You will find your identity in one mentor for a short time, and then in another as you try to copy those you admire, instead of being lead to find exactly who God called you to be.

A father calls out in this son his strengths and weaknesses to steer him in the right direction. A spiritual father helps do the same.

Moses and Jethro

There are so many jokes about in-laws out there, you might wonder whenever there is a positive relationship with one. Moses had fled Egypt at the age of 40, fleeing pharaoh after he murdered an Egyptian who had beaten a Hebrew. Moses not only left the only land he knew behind but his family and every living member of his people group — the Hebrews.

He settled among a tribe of the region, intermarried, had children among them, and took up his new profession herding sheep. He built a relationship with his father-in-law that became that of a spiritual father. We know that Jethro was a spiritual leader because he was the priest of their people. We know he was a spiritual father because of a time later after Moses lead the people out of Egypt.

Read this chapter, Exodus 18, to remind yourself of this relationship.

> *Now Jethro, the priest of Midian and father-in-law of Moses, heard of everything God had done for Moses and for his people Israel, and how the LORD had brought Israel out of Egypt.*
>
> *² After Moses had sent away his wife Zipporah, his father-in-law Jethro received her ³ and her two sons. One son was named Gershom, for Moses said, "I have become a foreigner in a foreign land"; ⁴ and the other was named Eliezer, for he said, "My father's God was my helper; he saved me from the sword of Pharaoh."*
>
> *⁵ Jethro, Moses' father-in-law, together with Moses' sons and wife, came to him in the wilderness, where he was camped near the mountain of God. ⁶ Jethro had sent word to him, "I, your father-in-law Jethro, am coming to you with your wife and her two sons."*
>
> *⁷ So Moses went out to meet his father-in-law and bowed down and kissed him. They greeted each other and then went into the tent. ⁸ Moses told his father-*

in-law about everything the LORD had done to Pharaoh and the Egyptians for Israel's sake and about all the hardships they had met along the way and how the LORD had saved them.

⁹ Jethro was delighted to hear about all the good things the LORD had done for Israel in rescuing them from the hand of the Egyptians. ¹⁰ He said, "Praise be to the LORD, who rescued you from the hand of the Egyptians and of Pharaoh, and who rescued the people from the hand of the Egyptians. ¹¹ Now I know that the LORD is greater than all other gods, for he did this to those who had treated Israel arrogantly." ¹² Then Jethro, Moses' father-in-law, brought a burnt offering and other sacrifices to God, and Aaron came with all the elders of Israel to eat a meal with Moses' father-in-law in the presence of God.

¹³ The next day Moses took his seat to serve as judge for the people, and they stood around him from morning till evening. ¹⁴ When his father-in-law saw all that Moses was doing for the people, he said, "What is this you are doing for the people? Why do you alone sit as judge, while all these people stand around you from morning till evening?"

¹⁵ Moses answered him, "Because the people come to me to seek God's will. ¹⁶ Whenever they have a dispute, it is brought to me, and I decide between the parties and inform them of God's decrees and instructions."

¹⁷ Moses' father-in-law replied, "What you are doing is not good. ¹⁸ You and these people who come to you will only wear yourselves out. The work is too heavy for you; you cannot handle it alone. ¹⁹ Listen now to me and I will give you some advice, and may God be with you. You must be the people's representative before God and bring their disputes to

him. ²⁰ Teach them his decrees and instructions, and show them the way they are to live and how they are to behave. ²¹ But select capable men from all the people—men who fear God, trustworthy men who hate dishonest gain—and appoint them as officials over thousands, hundreds, fifties and tens. ²² Have them serve as judges for the people at all times, but have them bring every difficult case to you; the simple cases they can decide themselves. That will make your load lighter, because they will share it with you. ²³ If you do this and God so commands, you will be able to stand the strain, and all these people will go home satisfied."

²⁴ Moses listened to his father-in-law and did everything he said. ²⁵ He chose capable men from all Israel and made them leaders of the people, officials over thousands, hundreds, fifties and tens. ²⁶ They served as judges for the people at all times. The difficult cases they brought to Moses, but the simple ones they decided themselves.

²⁷ Then Moses sent his father-in-law on his way, and Jethro returned to his own country.

There are several things to notice in these passages. Many people might skip the reference in verse 4 about the meaning of Moses' son's name: my father's God was my helper. Moses is referencing that God is the God of his own father. This points to how he was raised to believe in God and his family's impact on directing him toward God. That is the indeed the most worth task any parent can undertake. It also serves as a nice transition to the current father in Moses' life – his spiritual father, Jethro.

Notice in verse 7 the respect that Moses shows to Jethro.

He bows low and kissed him in respect. Jethro is more than a father-in-law. Moses respects him because of his relationship with God. Notice how often Moses, as the writer of Exodus, calls Jethro the priest of Midian. Jethro is much more than his father-in-law. Although God had His chosen people, the Hebrews, God was at work outside of those chosen people. Notice how God was at work in the lives of Melchizedek and Jethro — both priestly leaders of non-Hebrews. Also, look how God would soon be at work in a few hundred years in the lives of Rahab of Jericho, Ruth the Moabite, and the entire city of Nineveh. God was truly at work in ways that God alone knows. Moses recognized this special work of God through Jethro.

In verse 8, we see how Moses told Jethro everything about what had happened. The overall message was about God's goodness to them in delivering them from Egypt. But notice it also says that Moses talked about the hardships too. Moses let all the details be known. There was no glossing over the bad things to make himself look better or minimize the danger. He told Jethro everything.

How often do we have someone we can trust this completely with all the hardships as well? This is what you need in a spiritual father. Let's talk about what Jethro did when he heard all this.

I know many in-laws that are always critical of their son-in-law. No one can be good enough to marry their daughter, so they are going to criticize the son-in-law for everything that goes wrong. Not so for Jethro.

Jethro knew the focus was on what God had done to rescue His people. Notice Jethro's three-fold reaction. First, he was glad in his heart. Second, Jethro praised God. Third, he brought an offering in worship. This act recognized God's holiness and their sinfulness in the presence of God.

The next day Jethro observes Moses hard at work as a judge for all the people of Israel. It must have been a long line and an exhausting day. Jethro obviously did not like what he saw, but instead of criticizing, he asked Moses exactly what he was seeing. In other words, Jethro asked Moses to explain the situation.

When Moses explained, Jethro knew there was a problem, and he was not afraid to tell Moses why. Do we likewise have someone in our lives who can tell us: "What you are doing is not good"? Jethro went on to explain why and what Moses could do about it.

Jethro did Moses a huge favor by taking this approach. How many times do we tell people that what they are doing is not good, but we are not really able to tell them why? In those cases, it sounds like it is merely our opinion without support to back up our beliefs. That lacks convincing proof and can come across as offensive and arrogant, an "I know better than you do." Jethro instead gave a constructive solution.

To Moses' credit, he not only doesn't interrupt Jethro to explain with reasons, excuses, or clarifications. Moses listens. Not only does he respect what Jethro says, Moses adopts it into practice and finds that it is extremely helpful. The wisdom of Moses' spiritual father is clear, and listening to his advice pays off for Moses.

A spiritual father works just like this in your life. There will be words of encouragement and blessings, but they will also call out things in your life that are harmful to you and not in the best interests of the ministry God has called you to do.

You might call Jethro a double blessing in Moses' life as not only family — a father-in-law to him and grandfather to Moses' children — but also a spiritual father who helped guide Moses in his journey.

This reminds me again of Elisha. There are many who pray with a desire to receive what Elisha received, a double portion of the Spirit. However, such double portions are the inheritance of sons. Elisha received a double portion because he served Elijah, pursued him, learned his ways, and then received double the spirit of Elijah.

The lesson in the story of Elisha is that you must receive a mantle before you can give a mantle. You must study under another and be a disciple before you can be the rabbi.

I know many churches today who have found that they must do something similar with young parents. In the 21st century, we are so much more mobile than ever before. Kids don't always grow up and live right next door to their parents as they did in past generations. They might move away from their families and settle in another state — or half-way around the world for that matter. They may not have a parent close by who they can ask questions about raising their newborn. Churches set up this opportunity for older parents in their church, who have successfully navigated life with their kids, to mentor younger parents in the church. Usually, parents with kids 10 years or older are great because they have been through many of the same challenges, but are still young enough to relate culturally. In other words, there is less chance of getting a "back in my day" kind of speech. These relationships are life saving for many young parents.

If you are looking for a spiritual parent, look for someone who is possibly in your same profession and about 10 years older. It is fine to think about this as a person who is where you want to be in 10 years. The point is that they will be able to guide you in the next 10 years of your journey based on how they have successfully navigated those years as a growing follower of Jesus themselves. So, if you are a young pastor, look for a pastor who is further down the road from you.

However, don't fall trap to looking at a person in only one category. In other words, don't just pick a pastor because he has a bigger church or bigger offering. Pick someone because you notice several things you want to as well, a thriving relationship with God, to pray with a sense of passion and intimacy with God, an excellent counselor, power preacher, maturity in how he approaches life in the worst of times, and so on. Focus on who the person *is*, not what he *has*. Until you are willing to see that there are people in your life that are a gift to you, a voice of God to you, then you won't necessarily allow them to father you.

Chapter 9

Only the Qualified Should Touch You

"A man of deep understanding will give good advice, drawing it out from the well within." Proverbs 20:5 (The Passion Translation)

Stop allowing every Tom, Dick and Harry to lay hands on you and call you their spiritual son or daughter. Only the qualified should be putting their hand in your well, according to the text. Some people have been stagnated and hurt in the body of Christ because they continue to allow multiple unqualified, so-called spiritual fathers to lay hands on them and speak into and over their life.

Similar to our last chapter about not being someone's

spiritual father unless you have been someone's spiritual son, you should have a spiritual father who is also a spiritual son as well. Don't be afraid to ask about his past experiences, names of those he has been involved with, and what he has learned along the way.

I remember the first time I was preparing for a job interview, thinking of all the questions that the interviewer could ask me, when a wise person told me some good advice. A friend told me to remember that I was interviewing the company as much as they were interviewing me. At the time, I had no idea exactly what that meant because I really needed a job and probably would have said yes no matter what the working conditions were like. However, over the years, I have found that advice to be true.

A job interview or pastor search team meeting is all about finding the right person for the church or company that is searching. And things work out best when it is the best fit for both parties involved.

The truth is that a person can be a great worker or pastor, but that does not necessarily mean that the person is the best fit for the job. There are so many factors involved that make someone a good fit to be your spiritual father. Don't jump in too quickly without vetting your potential spiritual father.

Consider the following steps to finding your right spiritual father.

1. Pray diligently that God will provide the right spiritual father for you. God sometimes wants to teach

us through waiting patiently for His direction in our life. Ask God to give you a name.

2. Look around you. Has God already placed someone in your life who would be a natural fit as your spiritual parent? They would probably already be showing an interest in your life and ministry.

3. Start your search right there in your city. It may be tempting to go seek out your favorite pastor who lives in California, New York, or Chicago, but consider how someone close by can pour into your life more often from nearby.

Consider the following truths about spiritual fathering going back to the first patriarch, Father Abraham.

Truth 1: A spiritual father does not have to be a biological father.

We have already talked a lot about spiritual parenting and ways it is similar to parenting. But do you have to be a parent in order to be a spiritual parent?

When you think about it, you realize there are lots of examples of spiritual parents who were not parents — Jesus and Paul being two of the best examples of spiritual parents that we have who were not parents.

We cover Paul's relationship elsewhere in the book, but think of Jesus' relationship with the disciples that went deeper than that of a teacher. We see his love for Mary, Martha, Lazarus. Jesus weeps at this friend's death, the suffering of his sisters, and perhaps the unbelief surrounding him (John 11:35). Jesus also longed to take Jerusalem under his wings as noted in this passage:

> *How often I have longed to gather your children together, as a hen gathers her chicks under her wings, and you were not willing.*
>
> *(Matthew 23:37)*

Quite often Jesus had compassion for the masses and rebuked the Pharisees for their sin — characteristics that a spiritual parent must have through the day to day things that happen in life.

Abraham was such a spiritual father to Lot, even before he was a biological father. We see Abraham settling the dispute with Lot over the land (Gen. 13:5-13), going into battle to rescue Lot when his family was attacked (Gen. 14:1-16), and then asking God himself to save Lot and his family in the midst of the destruction of Sodom and Gomorrah (Gen. 18:16-33 and 19:29). He may have been acting as the family's kinsman-redeemer, but he did so with the spiritual parent hat on, hoping to bring Lot along in his maturity as one of the righteous.

Truth 2: A spiritual father will model his own deep relationship with God.

Abraham is at least three times in Scripture called God's friend (Isaiah 41:8; 2 Chronicles 20:7; James 2:3). It was widely known that God appeared to people various times and different ways, but very few get the treatment that Abraham receives. God appeared to Abraham several times and revealed to him God's own future plans.

Abraham even asks God to spare the righteous in Sodom in a way that most people dare not do — bargaining with God over the lives of the righteous, especially with his nephew Lot in mind. Genesis 29:19 shows us the result:

> *So when God destroyed the cities of the plain, he remembered Abraham, and he brought Lot out of the catastrophe that overthrew the cities where Lot had lived.*
>
> *(Genesis 29:19)*

Do you have a spiritual father who will stand in the gap for you before God?

Truth 3: A spiritual father will make mistakes.

God makes the first mention of the covenant to Abram here:

> *"I will make you into a great nation, and I will bless you; I will make your name great, and you will be a blessing.*
>
> *(Genesis 12:2)*

But a few verses later, we see Abram cooking up a lie to tell pharaoh to save his own skin.

> *Say you are my sister, so that I will be treated well for*

> *your sake and my life will be spared because of you.*
>
> *(Genesis 12:13)*

Later we see him do the same thing in a similar situation for fear of his life:

> *And Abraham said of Sarah his wife: "She is my sister."*
>
> *(Genesis 20:2)*

Abram certainly wasn't perfect, even if he was the friend of God. Your spiritual father won't be either.

Truth 4: A spiritual father will transmit his faith strengths (and mistakes) to you — the next generation.

Abraham's faith was great. He is one of the few in the Old Testament who is affirmed so thoroughly for his faith in God. Even in times of doubt, he didn't hold a grudge or worry. He went to God and asked:

> *[2] But Abram said, "Sovereign Lord, what can you give me since I remain childless and the one who will inherit my estate is Eliezer of Damascus?" [3] And Abram said, "You have given me no children; so a servant in my household will be my heir."*
>
> *(Genesis 15:2–3)*

God responded with affirmation of keeping that promise to Abraham.

> *"This man will not be your heir, but a son who is your own flesh and blood will be your heir." ⁵ He took him outside and said, "Look up at the sky and count the stars—if indeed you can count them." Then he said to him, "So shall your offspring[d] be."*
>
> (Genesis 15:4–5)

So what did Abraham do? If I were Abraham, I might have said, " OK, but God, when? Can you please tell me! I am dying here!"

But Abraham didn't question or try to pin God down. Instead, Abraham believed God.

> *Abram believed the L*ORD*, and he credited it to him as righteousness.*
>
> (Genesis 15:6)

Abraham believed God. He had that faith and took God's word for it.

Did Isaac learn that type of faith that Abraham had? Isaac had a similar encounter with God in a time of crisis, when there was a famine in the land. Let's see what happened.

> *The Lord appeared to Isaac and said, "Do not go down to Egypt; live in the land where I tell you to live. ³ Stay in this land for a while, and I will be with you and will bless you. For to you and your descendants I will give all these lands and will confirm the oath I swore to your father Abraham. ⁴ I will make your descendants as numerous as the stars*

> *in the sky and will give them all these lands, and through your offspring*[a] *all nations on earth will be blessed,*[b] *⁵ because Abraham obeyed me and did everything I required of him, keeping my commands, my decrees and my instructions." ⁶ So Isaac stayed in Gerar.*
>
> (Isaiah 26:2-6)

Indeed, Isaac had that faith. God told him what to do, reminded him of the faith of his father, and Isaac obeyed God. This is Isaac's moment of faith as well.

And almost on cue, we see in the very next passage:

> *When the men of that place asked him about his wife, he said, "She is my sister," because he was afraid to say, "She is my wife." He thought, "The men of this place might kill me on account of Rebekah, because she is beautiful."*
>
> (Isaiah 26:7)

Isaac made the same mistake his father did. He resorted to lying and deception to save himself.

So be aware that the sins of the father are passed on, just as the great examples of faith are. Be aware of the weaknesses of your parents, because they are likely to be your own as well.

Truth 5: God has a bigger plan than we can imagine. The goal is to trust God no matter what.

Abraham knew what it was like to be childless. God stepped in when Abraham was 75 and told him that he would be the father of a great nation.

> *All the land that you see I will give to you and your offspring[a] forever. ¹⁶ I will make your offspring like the dust of the earth, so that if anyone could count the dust, then your offspring could be counted.*
>
> *(Genesis 13:15-16)*

Abraham believed God.

> *Abram believed the LORD, and he credited it to him as righteousness.*
>
> *(Genesis 15:6)*

Abraham believed God. He had that faith and took God's word for it.

God kept His promise, despite Abraham fathering Ishmael. It was clear Abraham tried to make God's promise good on God's behalf. But God's plan was for Isaac. And God came through on that promised.

Probably the most difficult part of Abraham's parenting journey is when God asked Abraham then to be willing to sacrifice Isaac back to God. We read this description:

> *Some time later God tested Abraham. He said to him, "Abraham!"*
>
> *"Here I am," he replied.*
>
> *² Then God said, "Take your son, your only son,*

whom you love—Isaac—and go to the region of Moriah. Sacrifice him there as a burnt offering on a mountain I will show you."

³ Early the next morning Abraham got up and loaded his donkey. He took with him two of his servants and his son Isaac. When he had cut enough wood for the burnt offering, he set out for the place God had told him about. ⁴ On the third day Abraham looked up and saw the place in the distance. ⁵ He said to his servants, "Stay here with the donkey while I and the boy go over there. We will worship and then we will come back to you."

⁶ Abraham took the wood for the burnt offering and placed it on his son Isaac, and he himself carried the fire and the knife. As the two of them went on together, ⁷ Isaac spoke up and said to his father Abraham, "Father?"

"Yes, my son?" Abraham replied.

"The fire and wood are here," Isaac said, "but where is the lamb for the burnt offering?"

⁸ Abraham answered, "God himself will provide the lamb for the burnt offering, my son." And the two of them went on together.

⁹ When they reached the place God had told him about, Abraham built an altar there and arranged the wood on it. He bound his son Isaac and laid him on the altar, on top of the wood. ¹⁰ Then he reached out his hand and took the knife to slay his son. ¹¹ But the angel of the Lord called out to him from heaven, "Abraham! Abraham!"

"Here I am," he replied.

¹² "Do not lay a hand on the boy," he said. "Do not do anything to him. Now I know that you fear

God, because you have not withheld from me your son, your only son."

¹³ Abraham looked up and there in a thicket he saw a ram⁽ᵃ⁾ caught by its horns. He went over and took the ram and sacrificed it as a burnt offering instead of his son. ¹⁴ So Abraham called that place The Lord Will Provide. And to this day it is said, "On the mountain of the Lord it will be provided."

¹⁵ The angel of the Lord called to Abraham from heaven a second time ¹⁶ and said, "I swear by myself, declares the Lord, that because you have done this and have not withheld your son, your only son, ¹⁷ I will surely bless you and make your descendants as numerous as the stars in the sky and as the sand on the seashore. Your descendants will take possession of the cities of their enemies, ¹⁸ and through your offspring⁽ᵇ⁾ all nations on earth will be blessed,⁽ᶜ⁾ because you have obey me."

(Genesis 22:1–18)

Abraham went through the toughest trial of faith a parent could ever to be asked to do. But notice how calmly he points Isaac to the Lord's provision. "God will provide a lamb."

This response is the essence of spiritual parenting — being able to point children to God even in the midst of the worst trial imaginable. But this is more than being cool, calm, and collected. It is admirable to be a person whose feathers never get ruffled, but Abraham had so much more than that. Read the following from the faith chapter of the New Testament.

⁸ By faith Abraham, when called to go to a place he

would later receive as his inheritance, obeyed and went, even though he did not know where he was going. ⁹ By faith he made his home in the promised land like a stranger in a foreign country; he lived in tents, as did Isaac and Jacob, who were heirs with him of the same promise. ¹⁰ For he was looking forward to the city with foundations, whose architect and builder is God. ¹¹ And by faith even Sarah, who was past childbearing age, was enabled to bear children because she[b] considered him faithful who had made the promise. ¹² And so from this one man, and he as good as dead, came descendants as numerous as the stars in the sky and as countless as the sand on the seashore.

¹³ All these people were still living by faith when they died. They did not receive the things promised; they only saw them and welcomed them from a distance, admitting that they were foreigners and strangers on earth. ¹⁴ People who say such things show that they are looking for a country of their own. ¹⁵ If they had been thinking of the country they had left, they would have had opportunity to return. ¹⁶ Instead, they were longing for a better country—a heavenly one. Therefore God is not ashamed to be called their God, for he has prepared a city for them.

¹⁷ By faith Abraham, when God tested him, offered Isaac as a sacrifice. He who had embraced the promises was about to sacrifice his one and only son, ¹⁸ even though God had said to him, "It is through Isaac that your offspring will be reckoned."[c] ¹⁹ Abraham reasoned that God could even raise the dead, and so in a manner of speaking he did receive Isaac back from death.

This passage is amazing because it speaks to the faith of Abraham. Why did God make him wait? It built a faith in Abraham that was transforming. If Abraham and Sarah, who as this passage says "were as good as dead," could have a child in their old age, certainly God could raise Isaac back from the dead if He so chooses. Abraham had that kind of faith in God's promise.

This story is to help emphasize that you need a spiritual father who has been through the trials of life and has grown mighty in the faith of God. These are the kind of men who earn the right to be spiritual fathers.

Notice, it is not because they are perfect. No man is perfect. Only God is. Abraham is presented with all of his flaws. No sooner do we see Abraham demonstrate his allegiance to God by moving to the future promised land, than we see him lying down in Egypt trying to save his own skin from harm. Then, no sooner do we see God honor Abraham's faith than he tries to father the promised child with Hagar. Abraham had his flaws, but all the mistakes also contributed to his great faith and trust in God. Those are the type of men you want to go with you on your Mount Moriahs in life.

An immature spiritual parent can never mimic this faith, life experience, and trust in God. Only let those who are called by God to touch you speak into your life.

Chapter 10

Accepting the Spiritual Father, But Rejecting the Spiritual Mother

God never established organizations. He established relationships. If you look throughout the Bible, you find places where God called someone to fulfill a specific calling. He then gathered others around that person, both to support the one called to the work, and to receive a blessing from that person's ministry and guidance. In this, God established a system where each person who has been called is training up his or her replacement, giving that work perpetuity.

If you think about this, it matches God's character. John's first epistle tells us *"God is love"* (1 John 4:8,16), and love is relational. God doesn't send a machine to do His work, He didn't send an angel. He sent His Son. That Son, Jesus, built relationships with people here on Earth, preparing them to continue the ministry after He was crucified, rose from the dead, and returned to heaven. Think about how relational this verse is:

> *For God so loved the world that He gave His one and only Son, that whoever believes in Him shall not perish but have eternal life.*
>
> *(John 3:16)*

John 3:16 tells us about God's love and His sacrifice on our behalf so that we can have eternal life. He fought for our relationship by giving everything, and He was motivated to action because of how much he loved us.

The whole concept of spiritual fatherhood is relational. Spiritual sons seek out older, more experienced men, who can become their fathers, forming a relationship with them. It's not the fathers who seek out the sons; it's the sons who seek for those called to be their fathers.

There are always those who claim to be spiritual fathers and seek out those who will be their sons; men who are in it to build an organization, rather than to build true spiritual sons. They don't give to the sons, but rather take from them, usually financially.

With this being their motive, it's natural to ask whether they are truly to be called spiritual fathers. I can't really answer that, because I can't see their hearts. Only they and God know the answer to that question. But I would have to say they are either misunderstanding their calling, or they haven't really heard from God. Proceed with caution if you encounter a potential spiritual father like this.

Since this is a relationship, how the father and son relate to each other is of critical importance. On top of that, there is the issue of how the son fits into his new spiritual family. Entering into a relationship with a spiritual father also means entering into a relationship with anyone else the father is already in relationship with. Granted, that might not be as close of a relationship for you, but you will relate with each other nonetheless.

That can mean there are other spiritual sons and daughters you will encounter, but the most important of these relationships is with the spiritual mother. Many people forget about this relationship, acting as if the father-son relationship is the only one that matters, but that isn't so. To enter into a relationship with a father, but not the mother, puts the father into the unenviable position of divided loyalties. It forces him to choose continually between his wife and his spiritual son.

To understand how this compromises the husband-wife relationship, as well as how it compromises the father-son relationship, we must first understand what the Bible means when God declared

> *"The two shall be one flesh".*
> *(Gen 2:2 and Matt 19:5)*

There is only one sort of "one flesh" relationship referred

to in the Bible, that of a man and wife. Paul refers to the same thing in reference to *"joining with a harlot"* (1 Cor 6:16), but that is a mockery of what marriage is. In context, Paul is speaking of that from the viewpoint of how it harms the body of Christ. He is not in favor of it, but follows that up by admonishing the Corinthians to *"flee sexual immorality"*.

(1 Cor 6:18)

The idea of "one flesh" goes back to the creation. In Genesis 1, we find that God created man, whom he called "Adam."

> *Then God said, "Let Us make man in Our image, according to Our likeness; let them have dominion over the fish of the sea, over the birds of the air, and over the cattle, over all the earth and over every creeping thing that creeps on the earth." So God created man in His own image; in the image of God He created him; male and female He created them.*
>
> *(Genesis 1:26-27)*

The first thing to note here is that God's purpose was to create a being in His own image. That's not referring to a physical image; that's referring to a spiritual one. After all, God is a spirit, not a being made of flesh. So when God talked about creating Adam in His image, He's referring to the spirit of Adam.

Understanding that verse 26 allows us to understand verse 27, where it says that God created "him," "male and female" and "them." When it comes to flesh and blood humans, it's pretty much impossible for one person to fulfill all three of those terms. But in the spirit, it is possible. God created one being, whom He named Adam (man) and gave that being both male and female characteristics. As for the word "them," it doesn't exist in the original Hebrew, so we don't need to worry about it.

We know that God created only the spirit of man in chapter one, because He goes on to create man's body in chapter two and to "breathe" the spirit that he created in chapter one into it.

> *And the Lord formed man of the dust of the ground, and breathed into his nostrils the breath of life; and man became a living being.*
>
> *(Genesis 2:7)*

So now God has a body for the spirit He created in chapter one, into which He has placed the spirit, bringing that body to life. But at this point, there's just one body and one spirit. There aren't two; no man and wife. We see that happen later on in chapter two.

> *And the Lord God caused a deep sleep to fall upon Adam, and he slept: and he took one of his ribs, and closed up the flesh instead thereof. ^{22} And the rib which the Lord God had taken from man, made He a woman, and brought her unto the man.*
>
> *(Genesis 2:21-22)*

Every translation of the Bible I have seen says that God took a rib out of Adam, but if we look at that in Hebrew, we see the word *tsay-law*, which literally means "curved of the body." The same word can also be used architecturally to refer to a timber. So it's easy to see how it is translated as rib, even though there is no actual mention of bone in the definition of that word.

But in the Jewish scholarly tradition of biblical study, that word more correctly refers to "a part of the essence of who he was." That's a bit different. If we're talking essence of a person, we're talking about their soul and spirit, not their body. Since we know how God made man's body, and verse 22 tells us that He also made woman, it stands to reason that He made her body in much the same way that He made Adam, forming it out of the dust of the earth. Although, I'd have to say, He probably used a finer grade of dust.

So what did God need that *tsay-law* for? If he created Adam's spirit in the first place, and He made both bodies, why take that part of Adam out, in order to make the woman?

Remember where it said that God created man's spirit in His own likeness and that the sprit was both "him" and "male and female"? What God took out of Adam was the feminine part of him, the female part of his spirit. That's what He used as the essence of creating woman, placing it in a body that was specially crafted to match that spirit and soul.

God ended up with a masculine Adam in a masculine body and a feminine Adam in a feminine body. The male decided to call the female "woman" and named her "Eve."

Then, if this story isn't confusing enough, God brings the two of them together, saying that they shall be "one flesh."

> *Therefore shall man leave his father and his mother, and shall cleave unto his wife: they shall be one flesh.*
>
> *(Genesis 2:24)*

Ok, so why did He do that? It almost sounds like He made a mistake, but God doesn't make mistakes. Nevertheless, if He wanted them to be one, why didn't He leave both parts of the spirit in one body, just like He had it? He must have had a purpose.

> *How can one chase a thousand, and two put ten thousand to flight, unless their rock has sold them, and the Lord has surrendered them?*
>
> *(Deuteronomy 32:30)*

There's a word for this, when people working together are able to multiply their effectiveness. It's called *synergy*. God's purpose in dividing His creation and bringing them back together was to make them better. In doing this, He made it possible for them to accomplish more. Not just more now that there are two people and could get twice as much done, but a multiplication, so that they could do the work of 10, 20, perhaps even 50.

Then God says:

So then, they are no longer two but one flesh. Therefore, what God has joined together, let not man put asunder.
(Matthew 19:6)

That's it. It's permanent. At least, that's God's intent, even if there are those who might care to tear that marriage asunder.

But here's the thing from the viewpoint of being a spiritual son ... you don't want to be the one to tear that marriage asunder, even if it's just a little bit. How can you or I expect God to bless us, when we do things that go against His will? Isn't that what we'd be doing, if we were to try and have a relationship with a spiritual father, while ignoring the relationship with his wife, the woman who should be the spiritual mother? Wouldn't that be a form of tearing their marriage asunder?

In dividing the spirit and soul of Adam, God gave different characteristics to the man and woman. This was no accident; He knew that for the ability of His creation to be multiplied, they would each need to fulfill a specific purpose in that relationship. By giving them different characteristics, He ensured that they would approach every situation from different viewpoints, increasing their ability to deal with that situation effectively. If one partner's way of dealing with a situation is ineffective, the other partner's approach will probably work.

This is perhaps most easily seen in the difference between a mother's love and a father's love. A mother's nature is to protect, even if she has to put herself in harm's way to do so. This is best illustrated by a mother bird covering her babies with her own body to protect them from a forest fire. That mother may very likely die, but her babies will probably survive.

The father takes a different approach and while a he may die protecting his children from that fire, he would not die the same way. Rather, he would die fighting the fire and trying to get his children out of it. He might throw his body onto the fire, so that his children could walk over it, but he wouldn't just stay there, being burnt, trying to be a shield around them.

Or perhaps we could look at it this way. If a child can't swim, their mother will try to keep them out of the water, or insist that they stay where the water is shallow, so that they can't drown. A father, on the other hand, will throw that child in the deep water, where they can't touch bottom, so that they have to learn how to swim. The father's way is seen as cruel by the mother, but when all is said and done, the child can swim and is protected from drowning, even when his mother isn't there to tell him to stay in the shallow water.

Which is the greater love? A mother's love is touted as being all-supreme, but I contest that both are necessary. When a child receives only a mother's love, they miss what they need from the father. Likewise, when they receive love only from a father, without the mother, there are other things they'll miss.

Since the two are one flesh, then if one is called into the ministry, they are both called. They might not both fulfill the same role in that ministry, but they are in it together, nevertheless. Whatever gifts and talents they have received from the Lord will complement each other, fulfilling something that the other partner doesn't have or can't do. That's being one flesh.

From the spiritual son's point of view, each of those spiritual parents provides something different. While the son might be more interested in what the spiritual father has to offer, they might actually have a greater need for what the mother has to offer. Many times what we're seeking is not what we really need. We don't always see our needs, but God knows what they are.

There's also a difference in how spiritual parents will pray for their son. Have you ever noticed that when the pastor calls for intercession, it's mostly women who show up? Why is that? It's because intercession is mostly defensive, the realm of the female, not offensive, which is more likely to be the realm of the male.

Let me clarify here. We tend to use the terms "intercession" and "spiritual warfare" interchangeably. But they're not the same thing. As I just said, intercession is defensive in nature, while spiritual warfare is offensive. Men have been given the characteristics of aggressiveness and violence for warfare, but they're not well suited to intercession. That falls closer to a mother's heart and her love.

In the book of Deuteronomy, one of the many unusual commands which God gives the nation of Israel is the following:

> *When a man has taken a new wife, he shall not out to war or be charged with any business; he shall be free at home one year, and bring happiness to his*

wife whom he has taken.

(Deuteronomy 24:5)

Sounds a bit strange, doesn't it? In fact, it sounds pretty much impossible to do, at least in our modern society, rushing here and there with so much to do. But what would happen if we did that? What if we actually had a "honey-year" instead of a "honeymoon?"

One thing that would happen is that when the man went off to war, something we saw quite often in the history of Israel, his wife would be on her knees, back home, praying for God to protect her husband. She would be his spiritual shield, defending him by constantly surrounding him with prayer, while he was on the offensive, fighting that war.

We all need both of these characteristics in our lives. As spiritual sons and daughters, we need someone who is praying God's protection over us, while at the same time, we have someone else who is going to battle against the enemy on our behalf. When we have both, we stand a greater chance of being able to walk in the fullness of God's victory.

Rejecting a spiritual mother, while accepting the spiritual father (or vice-versa) is refusing a gift that God the Father has prepared for you. You may not know what that woman can do for you, but that doesn't minimize the importance of her actions. For that matter, you may never see it with your natural eyes, but that doesn't mean it's not there. Some of the greatest blessings from God end up being things we can't see with our natural eyes.

Long before you were born, God knew His plan for your life.

> *Before I formed you in the womb I knew you; before you were born I sanctified you; I ordained you a prophet to the nations.*
>
> *(Jeremiah 1:5)*

While that verse is specifically talking about the prophet Jeremiah, we can take it to be talking about us as well. God has called each and every one of us, long before we were born, even those who feel no calling to full-time ministry.

If God has called us, hasn't He also made provision to go with that calling? I certainly believe so. If that's the case, then the spiritual father and spiritual mother that He has prepared for us are part of that provision too. It doesn't matter if we like them, just as long as they are what we need.

We have a tendency to think that everything God does for us is going to make us feel good and make us happy. But that's just not so. I'm sorry to tell you that God's ultimate goal in our lives isn't to make us happy; it's to remake us into the image of Jesus Christ.

> *For those that He foreknew, He also predestined to be conformed to the image of His Son, that He might be the firstborn among many brethren.*
>
> *(Romans 8:29)*

I think it's safe to say that the curriculum for that course isn't going to be easy. Being transformed into the image of Christ will require a lot of things to be removed from our lives and a lot of new things added in. Some of those things that are removed are going to hurt to lose, but they will ultimately be to our own benefit. Likewise, some of the things that God wants to put into our lives are going to hurt going in, until we get used to them.

So how will God do this? Mostly through the people in our lives. We might think we're looking for a spiritual father to help us, but we really don't understand the fullness of what that help is going to be. Just like a natural father disciplines and corrects his children, we must expect that our spiritual fathers will discipline and correct us too. That won't always be enjoyable.

But it's not just the spiritual father who will do that. It's the spiritual mother as well. As I just said, they're a team. God called them into the ministry together. So we must see her as part of that process, even if she rubs us the wrong way.

Actually, rubbing us the wrong way might be just what we need. We've all got a few rough edges on us that need to be rubbed off. That takes someone who is willing to do the rubbing. They might not like it any more than we do, but they'll recognize the need to rub and keep on rubbing, until you and I shine like a gem.

> *You also, as living stones, are being built up a spiritual house, a holy priesthood, to offer up spiritual sacrifices acceptable to God through Jesus Christ.*

(1 Peter 2:5)

Have you ever seen how buildings are built by stone? I'm not talking about stone that comes to the job site nice and neat from a stonecutter somewhere. I'm talking about stone that's quarried on site and cut by hand — the old way, the way they built for thousands of years before modern power tools existed.

In the Middle Ages, stone cutters worked by using pressure to split stones. Starting from whatever opening they could find or create, they would drive wedges into the stone, until the stone split. Smaller breaks would be created in the stone in the same way, applying pressure to the stone in order to get pieces to flake off. Once the stone was shaped, it would be smoothed by rubbing it with harder stones, stone against stone and allowing those harder stones to grind off the rough spots.

But that was during the Iron Age. Mankind was carving stone long before that by rubbing soft stones with hard ones. The Olmeca people of Mesoamerica created massive figures this way, some three meters tall and weighing several tons. Yet they were all created by rubbing stone with stone.

If stones had feelings, it would have hurt to be a stone, being constantly rubbed the wrong way as pieces of you broke off, all with the intent of making you look the way someone else wants you to look.

This is what's happening with us as "living stones." We too are rubbing each other the wrong way, not just to irritate, but to show us where our rough spots are. Each time we go "ouch" from being rubbed the wrong way, God wants us to look at our own hearts and see why we are saying ouch, where we are wrong, rather than looking at the other person and say that there's something wrong with them.

What if God has selected that spiritual mother for you because He knew that she would rub you the wrong way? What if that rubbing is just what you need, so that you can find the areas you need to grow? What if that's God's perfect will for you?

Job said to his wife, in the midst of his affliction:

> *You speak as one of the foolish women speaks. Shall we indeed accept good from God, and shall we not accept adversity?*
>
> *(Job 2:10)*

Yet many Christians do just the opposite, accepting the good from God, while rejecting the bad that God allows into our lives. They reject the very person who God has ordained to bring about a positive change in their lives, just because they don't like them. Then they expect others to go along with their decision. If they don't, their response usually is, "You don't love me."

A spiritual father and spiritual mother are two sides of the same coin. You cannot have one without the other. Yes, there are cases where a spiritual father may be unmarried, but that can change at any time. Would you break covenant with that spiritual father, just because they wed?

God's ways always bring balance to our lives. This is no exception. The old saying about "opposites attract" is true. So the chances are that if you find a spiritual father who you are comfortable with, his wife will be the opposite personality, and you won't be comfortable with her. What will you do then?

Since entering into a relationship with a spiritual father is a covenant relationship, we must consider it to be a life-long commitment. Nothing else will do. Without that covenant commitment, we won't receive correction. If we won't receive correction, he really isn't a father after all.

Since the spiritual father is in a covenant relationship with his wife, that means that the spiritual sons and daughters are actually in covenant with both of them, regardless of whether they want it that way or not. They are a family, committed to love one another, be there for one another, and constantly seek the best for one another.

The interesting thing is that you can love family members without necessarily liking them. All children go through phases where they don't like their parents. Yet, that doesn't stop those adults from being their parents. They will still speak into that child's life, correct that child, and do everything they can to meet that child's needs, while waiting for the day that their child gets over being mad at them and decides to allow love to overcome their hate.

That's part of being a parent, and, fortunately, mothers are very good at it. While their child's anger and hatred always hurts them, their love overcomes that pain. So they wait for the day when they can feel their child's love once again.

Rejecting your mother, whether spiritual or natural, is rejecting your life-giver. In the natural, the mother gives life to that child, so what makes us think that it's not the same in the spiritual? Fathers don't give birth to new spiritual children, nor give birth to their ministries; they just officiate over them. It takes a mother to give birth, and that's what makes her a mother.

Are you willing to destroy your own calling in life, by rejecting the spiritual mother God has selected for you, or will you let that living stone rub against you, helping to give birth to the good that God wants in your life?

Chapter 11

Like Father, Like Son

There's a lot of truth to the old phrase, "like father, like son;" but more importantly, there's a great need for it as well. Sons need a father to look up to and emulate, so that they can learn how to be men. This is true both in the spiritual and in the natural. One of the greatest services a spiritual father performs for his spiritual son is to demonstrate what a godly man looks and acts like, so they can have an example to emulate.

We humans are great imitators, it's a learning mechanism built into us, and central to learning some of life's most important skills; things like walking and talking. Babies begin to walk, because they see their parents, siblings and others walking. Watching them, they realize that they should be walking too, so they try. It is through their constant trial and error that they learn to walk.

Pretty much all babies learn to walk. The only ones who don't have some underlying medical problem that prevents them from doing so. But they won't learn on their first try, or even on their hundredth try. That's okay, they'll keep on trying, simply because they see others doing so. That's all the motivation they need. Eventually, they will succeed.

While imitation is an essential learning element for babies and toddlers, we don't lose that ability as we grow older. Nor do we lose the desire to emulate those we see, especially those we admire. The question then becomes, who is it that we are emulating and are they a good example to us?

The Apostle Paul learned fatherhood not by raising natural children, but by raising spiritual ones. We really have no idea how many of those there were, just the names of a couple of special ones; Timothy and Titus. There may very well have been many more, but at least in the case of these two young men, Paul clearly adopted them as sons and they likewise adopted him as their father.

In this, Paul demonstrated the Christian life and godly character not through the classroom, but through how he lived each and every day. As he traveled and worked, his sons were by his side. They saw the example of his life, which was ultimately much more important than any lesson he could write or teach.

While we are not given the opportunity to watch Paul interact with either of these two sons, we know through his letters that he did, especially with Timothy, who he apparently wrote to more than Titus. Not only do we have the text of two letters that Paul wrote to Timothy, but each of those is longer than the one letter we have that he sent to Titus. Additionally, we have what he said to the Corinthians about Timothy.

> *Therefore I urge you to imitate me. ¹⁷For this reason I have sent to you Timothy, my son whom I love, who is faithful in the Lord. He will remind you of my way of life in Christ Jesus, which agrees with what I teach everywhere in every church.*
>
> *(1 Corinthians 4:16-17)*

The Apostle Paul in principle is saying when you get my spiritual son Timothy, it's just like you are getting me. If this was said by anyone but the Apostle Paul, it would be easy to call it prideful. But we have to remember who was saying it; a man who had given up everything for the Lord. Paul had been a Pharisee and member of the Sanhedrin before his Damascus Road experience. Yet we see through his epistles that he lost the pride that had sustained him as a Pharisee and had become a meek man.

This humbling didn't happen overnight. You can actually map it out, through the epistles that he wrote and how he talks about himself in those epistles. The man who started out so arrogant that he went to other cities to persecute Christians under the authority of the Sanhedrin, became one of the humblest Christians who has ever lived.

Having become humble, Paul knew the value of having his sons follow his example and imitating his way of life. It's clear from this verse, that he has given Timothy a very specific mission in visiting them, to remind them of how Paul lived in agreement with what he wrote.

How could Timothy best do that? By demonstrating it to them through his own life. While the text doesn't actually say so, it's reasonable to presume that Paul sent Timothy with this message because Paul saw a lot of himself in his spiritual son. While there were others that he could have sent, the epistles and the book of Acts speak of several companions he had through the years, he was very specific in who he chose, sending the one man who best knew how he himself lived.

But, there's another lesson even more important in this verse. That is how Paul's life and his teaching were in agreement. He wasn't telling people "do as I say, not as I do," he was saying "let me show you how to do what I say." There's a huge difference between the two.

A true spiritual father knows that his sons will follow after his example, more than after his words. They may not even remember his words. But you can be sure that they will always remember his character and actions. Therefore, he strives to make his words and actions line up in agreement. More than that, he strives to model Christ-likeness for them. For it is only through modeling this that he is truly teaching.

> [16] *So I urge and implore you, be imitators of me.*
>
> [17] *For this very cause I sent to you Timothy, who is my beloved and trustworthy child in the Lord, who will recall to your minds my methods of proceeding and course of conduct and way of life in Christ, such as I teach everywhere in each of the churches.*

(1 Corinthians 4:16-17 Amplified Bible, Classic Edition)

Something else in the text I believe many overlook that I would love to highlight. Many think God's best for spiritual sonship is learned through some type of theological seminary, instead of the school of hard knocks, and that is submitting to a spiritual father in ministry. I believe that Bible college and or seminary has is place in a making a difference in a person's life when we send our future leaders to a theological seminary or Bible college. I too have attended and graduated from several. I think it's a false expectation and a violation of the aforementioned text to think that it's the best route to prepare someone for ministry.

Recommending someone to go to Bible college to prepare them for next level in ministry is setting them up for failure. Literally, what you are doing is sending them out to be raised by surrogates who don't have spiritual fathers themselves, but have college degree. A child without a father is an illegitimate child, or a bastard (no, that isn't a curse word). Sadly, most churches and ministries today are started by spiritual bastards and they perpetual the cycle on to the next generations.

How can a college professor, who does not have a spiritual father, or who is not a spiritual father himself know how to father others? They can't, shucks! Timothy watched his spiritual father closely. Timothy had his spiritual father spirit on him and it qualified him to be sent out in his spiritual father's stead. He also had pure motives, Lord have mercy, and wasn't going to do anything that he hasn't seen his spiritual parents do before. Listen to my heart please, a spiritual father is there to console, impart wisdom, correct, and instruct. A true spiritual father is always there for his child, in the good times and especially the bad. However, when a pastor, or minister is raised in the sterile atmosphere of a Bible school without a spiritual father, they look at their ministry as work, not as a family relationship.

It is no wonder that most of our churches are started as church splits. Without a father/son relationship, there is no reason to stay working with another minister. There is no expectancy of receiving the blessing of the spiritual father. There is no covenant of love. There is only a selfish desire to do one's own thing, even at the cost of hurting a spiritual father and spiritual mother. So, these young ministers actually are only looking for an opportunity to start their own ministry. If that comes at the cost of someone else's ministry, it doesn't matter to them. Instead of seeing their actions as being wrong, they convince themselves that they are doing what is necessary and best for the people they are taking from that church. This is a work of rebellion, and God cannot bless anything that starts in rebellion.

If a ministry that starts in rebellion ends up receiving God's blessings, it is because at some point along the line they realize their error, and repent before the Lord, and come into proper alignment with the Word of God submitting to a spiritual father and mother, shucks.

This is the key to spiritual fathers and mothers in the ministry. Recent statistics say that ninety percent of pastors feel that their Bible school training didn't prepare them for the ministry! Why? Because what is being taught in Bible college and seminary is only the theory of ministry, not the fact of it. Just because someone knows theory doesn't mean that they can apply it, hello somebody. Nor does it mean that the theory works. All it means is that they've learned a bunch of things to pass courses with a least a "C" or better, shucks. Things, that unfortunately, according to 90% of the pastors out there, aren't useful in their day-to-day ministry.

I am a graduate of Bible college and seminary, and I promise you that what I've learned from my spiritual dad and mom and the anointing that was transferred unto my life prepared me for ministry far greater than Bible college and seminary.

There are many other examples of spiritual fatherhood, as a manner of training in the Bible. Here are a few key examples:

Moses & Joshua – In Exodus, chapter 33, verses 7 to 11, we find that Moses pitched his tent outside of the camp and used it as a place to meet with God. At the end of verse 11, we find this interesting phrase *"his servant Joshua, the son of Nun, a young man, departed not out of the tabernacle."* Joshua started out as Moses' servant, learning from Moses, staying in the presence of the Lord, and being prepared for leadership. At the end of Moses' life, in Deuteronomy, chapter 34, verse 9, Moses laid hands on this same Joshua, and anointed him to become the next leader over Israel.

Elijah & Elisha – This is probably the greatest example of spiritual fatherhood in the Old Testament. In First Kings, chapter 19, verse 16, God commanded the prophet Elijah to anoint Elisha to be a prophet. When Elijah found Elisha, he cast his mantle over Elisha. Between that time, and Second Kings, chapter 2, when Elijah was taken up to heaven, Elisha stayed with Elijah, and served him. He then received the "double portion" of Elijah's spirit to become prophet after Elijah.

The Aaronic Priesthood – When God commanded Moses to anoint his brother, Aaron, as high priest, he also anointed his sons as priests (Ex 28:1). God commanded that only the descendants of Aaron would be the priests of Israel. These priests raised up their sons to take their place in the ministry, training them, and preparing them for the work of ministering to the Lord, and to His people.

The concept of spiritual fatherhood is one in which, just as the prophets did with the sons of the prophets, a minister or leader takes another under his wing to train and equip them for the work the Lord has called them to do.

During this time of "walking together" the spiritual son is able to observe the life, character, and ministry of his spiritual father. Through this, he learns not only book knowledge, but also how to apply this knowledge in various ministry situations. Even more important than this, however, is that he is able to observe the character of his spiritual father and imitate him, developing his spirit man.

As they are "walking together" the spiritual father is able to observe the life, character, and giftings of his spiritual son. Through this, he is able to help correct and discipline his son, building the proper character and fruits of the Spirit within him. He can also help recognize the specific calling that God has for the life of his son, and direct and prepare him for that specific work.

By working with this type of system, we aren't preparing "cookie cutter" ministers, who have a general knowledge of the Bible, but no specific direction for their lives. Instead, we sharpen the young minister just as a sword is sharpened, making him ready to pierce the darkness in a specific place and manner.

The time of training will vary from individual to individual, depending upon their biblical knowledge, character, and when they are able to release to go speak in your stead. Their specific calling will play a part in this as well, as some may require more preparation than others. Another part of this training will be that the son has opportunities to minister on his own, with the oversight of his spiritual father. Jesus anointed his disciples and sent them out to minister on their own. No matter how much we learn in a classroom setting, or by watching someone else, without the opportunity to practice doing it, that knowledge doesn't become heart knowledge, but only head knowledge.

When it is time for the spiritual son to step out in his own ministry, both the father and son will recognize it. Instead of leaving in rebellion, he will be able to leave with his spiritual father's blessing and support.

This point of leaving doesn't mean that the relationship ends, just that it moves to a new phase. Just as a natural son leaving the home stays in a relationship with his parents, so too do these spiritual sons need to stay connected to their spiritual fathers.

In a way, the ongoing father/son relationship is more important after the son starts in ministry, than before. This is the time when he will especially need the wisdom and experience of his father. Many of the previously taught lessons will suddenly take on a whole new light, and may need some review and further explanation. Mare than that, the son will need the ongoing prayers of his father to keep him strong, focused, and protected.

Let's go back and look at the relationship between Elijah and Elisha again. As I said, this is probably the best example of spiritual fatherhood in the Bible, and there are several things we can glean from their lives.

To start with, let's look at how Elijah started fathering Elisha.

> *And Jehu the son of Nimshi shalt thou anoint to be king over Israel: and <u>Elisha</u> the son of Shaphat of Abel-meholah <u>shalt thou anoint to be prophet in thy room</u>.[19] So he departed thence, and found Elisha the son of Shaphat, who was plowing with twelve yoke of oxen before him, and he with the twelfth: and Elijah passed by him, and <u>cast his mantle upon him</u>. [20] And he left the oxen, and ran after Elijah, and said, Let me, I pray thee, kiss my father and my mother, and then I will follow thee. And he said unto him, Go back again: for what have I done to thee? [21] And he returned back from him, and took a yoke of oxen, and slew them, and boiled their flesh with the instruments of the oxen, and gave unto the people, and*

they did eat. <u>Then he arose, and went after Elijah, and ministered unto him.</u>

One of the benefits of the spiritual father/son relationship is a transference of the anointing. Elijah was directed to give the anointing that he had to Elisha. That doesn't mean that Elijah would no longer have the anointing, but that it would become multiplied in another minister's life and ministry. Later on, Elisha asked for the "double portion" of Elijah's spirit, which is the same thing as asking for a double portion of his anointing (2 Ki 2:9). We'll talk more about this in a minute.

Notice how Elijah obeyed God in this instance. Verse 19, of 1 Kings, chapter 19 says, *"he left there and found Elisha..."* He didn't wait for Elisha to come to him, he went and found the man who God told him to find. This doesn't mean that God will always do things this way, but it does tell us that the person, or people who we are to father won't necessarily always be someone in our congregation.

When Elijah found Elisha, verse 19 says he *"cast his mantle upon him."* This is important. The mantle, which was literally Elijah's prayer shawl, is the outer garment that a Jew wears. Just as a jacket, it is a sign of authority. When Elijah put his prayer shawl on Elisha, it was a symbol of giving his authority to Elisha in obedience to God's command.

However, we don't see anywhere in the scripture where Elijah poured oil upon Elisha to anoint him. Why not? Because the anointing of an individual flows onto their "mantle." When Elijah put his mantle upon Elisha, he not only gave him his authority, but his anointing as well.

This passage of scripture ends by saying that Elisha *"went after Elijah, and ministered unto (or, served) him."* Elisha received his training for the ministry by walking with Elijah, serving him, watching him, speaking with him, and ministering with him.

The first to recognize this was the sons of the prophets who were on the other side of the river watching all this. They instantly accepted him, and looked to him for leadership.

> *<u>He took up also the mantle of Elijah that fell from him</u>, and went back, and stood by the bank of Jordan; ¹⁴ And he took the mantle of Elijah that fell from him, and smote the waters, and said, Where is the LORD God of Elijah? and when he also had smitten the waters, they parted hither and thither: and Elisha went over. ¹⁵ And <u>when the sons of the prophets which were to view at Jericho saw him, they said, The spirit of Elijah doth rest on Elisha.</u> And they came to meet him, and bowed themselves to the ground before him.*
>
> *(2 Ki 2:13-15)*

Notice that Elijah smote the waters twice in verse 14. The first time, it appears that nothing happened. However, after he said, *"Where is the Lord God of Elijah?"* and smote the waters again, they parted, just as they had for Elijah. This was God's seal of confirmation on Elisha's position, anointing, and authority.

If the example of Elijah and Elisha is representative of what God wants, than we should see a doubling of anointing in each spiritual generation. However, I don't know of anywhere in the world where this is happening today.

What we are doing today is only training ministers, instead of raising spiritual sons and spiritual daughters. As you can see from this study, there is an incredible difference between the two.

If you call yourself a spiritual father and you don't raise up spiritual sons and spiritual daughters, you are spiritual eunuchs. In Leviticus 21, God gave Moses a list of defects that would prevent Aaron's descendants from serving in the priesthood (Lev 21:17-21). Amongst this list is mentioned, "damaged testicles" (or in some translations "eunuchs"). Physically, this means an inability to reproduce, and spiritually it means the same thing. Literally, God has declared in the law, that those who don't reproduce spiritually are unfit to be ministers.

I don't know about you, but I want to see the church grow and be filled with the presence and glory of the Lord. I want my spiritual sons (and natural ones as well) to raise up and take the ministry of the Lord to new levels. I want to see all of God's plan fulfilled here on the earth. Just as Jesus prayed in the Lord's prayer:

> *"Thy kingdom come. Thy will be done in earth, as it is in heaven".*
>
> *(Mt 6:10)*

> *Behold, I will send you Elijah the prophet before the coming of the great and dreadful day of the LORD* [6] *And he shall turn the heart of the (spiritual) fathers to the (spiritual) children (or sons), and the heart of the (spiritual) children (or sons) to their (spiritual) fathers, lest I come and smite the earth with a curse.*
>
> *(Malachi 4:5-6 annotations mine)*

Come Elijah, under the direction of the Holy Spirit, as Malachi prophesied, and turn the hearts of the spiritual fathers, back to their spiritual sons. So that our land may not be cursed, but blessed with the knowledge of the glory of the Lord. Amen.

Paul was the ultimate father figure, founding and fathering much of the Early Church. He understood this necessity to be an example of Christ to them, and set aside all his earthly accolades, so that he might demonstrate Jesus to them.

In Paul's second letter to the Corinthians, he takes a chapter and a half to boast about himself, calling himself a "madman" for doing so. He felt forced to do this, because his ministry had come under attack. But it was more than just a defense of his ministry; there was a point to it all, because he ends this strange discourse by saying:

> *Therefore I will boast all the more gladly of my weakness, so that the power of Christ may rest upon me.* [10] *For the sake of Christ, then, I am content with weaknesses, insults, hardships, persecutions, and calamities. For when I am weak, then I am strong.*
>
> *(2 Corinthians 12:9-10)*

Paul cast aside whatever greatness that he might have had, in order to become weak and to glory in that weakness. He knew something that we all need to learn. That is, Christ can accomplish more through us, than we can accomplish for Him. We just need to get out of the way.

Our greatest purpose in life isn't the ministry that we have but the ministry we allow Christ to have through us. The better a job we can do of that, the more we will accomplish for the kingdom. We must teach our spiritual sons to do the same, so that they might even surpass us in what they can allow Christ to accomplish through them.

So, why would Paul take so much time to brag about his "credentials" all while telling the reader that he was acting as a fool?

Paul made a choice in his life, deciding that knowing Christ was more important than anything else. It was an important message he wanted his sons and daughters to learn. By taking the time to brag to them about his past, he was increasing the relative value of his relationship with Christ in every line. Each thing he had renounced for Christ, showed how much more valuable that relationship was to him.

But that's not all he was doing. This boasting follows a chapter where he is defending his ministry, as it had come under attack from others who called themselves ministers. These people didn't have the same heart for Paul's spiritual sons and daughters that he himself had. One proof of his love for his spiritual children was what he had given up for them.

This was a message to all Paul's sons and daughters,

throughout all the churches, not just those who were special to him. Although we think of Timothy and Titus as his sons, we really can't limit that title to only them. In reality, every member of every congregation that Paul founded was part of his family; his sons and daughters. He understood that responsibility and took it seriously.

There is no question that Paul understands the importance of imitation. In his second letter to the Thessalonians, he reminds and admonishes them:

> *For you yourself know how you ought to imitate us, because we were not idle when we were with you.*
>
> *(2 Thessalonians 3:7)*

While that verse is making reference to food, his working to provide for his own needs, rather than expecting others to take care of him, it readily applies to all areas of life. Paul doesn't separate his spiritual life from his natural one. They are both part of the same.

He lived the Christian life in everything he did, as well as preaching and teaching about it. You never see a place where he sets aside his life in Christ, so that he could enjoy the ball game or go for a night on the town.

More than anything else, the life Paul lived was his credentials. This should be our example as well. Many ministers point to their works as their credentials, whether it be the messages they preach, the size of their ministry of the miracles the Holy Spirit performs though them. But none of those actually prove that they are great ministers or even that they are great believers. The true measure of any minister is how they live when they're not in the pulpit. In another place, Paul tells the church:

> *What you have learned and received and heard and seen in me – practice these things and the God of peace will be with you.*
>
> *(Philippians 4:9)*

Practice which things? The things that they have seen and heard from Paul. Why? So that the peace of God would be with them. In other words, Paul's godly life is a path towards peace. If his spiritual sons wanted peace, they should get it the same way he did, through the life that he lived.

This becomes even more interesting, when we take that verse in context, seeing what is written before it:

> *Finally, brothers, whatever is true, whatever is honorable, whatever is just, whatever is pure, whatever is lovely, whatever is commendable, if there be any excellence, if there is anything worthy of praise, think about these things.*
>
> *(Philippians 4:8)*

Paul makes it clear both what to think and what to do. While he doesn't exactly say it, the inference is that he is thinking those things he admonishes others to think, making that part of what they are to do to live a godly life as his spiritual children. Just as God desires to reproduce Himself in us, so too Paul has that same desire to reproduce himself in all those he considers his spiritual sons.

As spiritual fathers, we should have that same desire. Not only that, but we should understand the gravity of the responsibility we take on ourselves, when we accept the role of a spiritual father. In doing so, we are saying before our God that we will do our best to immolate Him, so that we can show our spiritual sons how to do the same.

As spiritual sons, we should only look for spiritual fathers who demonstrate Christlikeness and godliness to us. If we can't see Him in them, then they aren't going to help us in our own walk. Oh, they might be great teachers; but there's a huge difference between being a teacher of the word, and being a spiritual father. The teacher doesn't have the same level of responsibility, even though they should also take it upon themselves to display a godly character.

> *For though you might have ten thousand instructors in Christ, yet you do not have many fathers; for in Christ Jesus I have begotten you through the gospel.*
> *(1 Corinthians 4:15)*

Being at teacher doesn't make one a spiritual father, although all teachers can be spiritual fathers, following in Paul's example. Nor does being a preacher make anyone a spiritual father. Pastors can't automatically consider themselves to be spiritual fathers either, although if any of the five-fold ministry should have the nature of the spiritual father, it is the pastor. Becoming a spiritual father is accepting a unique mantle, one that is not automatically conferred with any other ministry.

Many who are not truly fathers do not understand the impact of their own fatherhood. They don't understand how their spiritual children will follow in their footsteps. Not in the sense of fulfilling their ministry or taking it over once the spiritual father retires, but in the sense of how that relationship will mold the heart and character of the son. Because they take that lightly, they consign their sons to make the same mistakes they have made.

Our faults will reproduce themselves in our sons and daughters, no matter how hard we try to make it otherwise. They truly do follow our example better than they follow our words. So if we are not living a good example before them, we will see the results in their lives.

There are countless examples like this, although we won't see them if we don't take the time to look for them. We tend to accept such things as happenstance or coincidence, ignoring the greater spiritual implications of them. Yet that's not something we should ignore. The truth will eventually come out.

However, we shouldn't only focus on the negative side; there's a positive side to that coin. For where a spiritual father is strong, he will pass that on to his sons as well. If he is generous, he'll teach his sons to be generous too. If he's a worshipper, they'll learn how to worship. If he has hard-earned wisdom from the Word of God, they'll learn that same wisdom and if he unashamed of the gospel, they will be as well.

These attributes won't necessarily carry across to all who

receive from that ministry, only those who are spiritual sons. Just as not everyone who listened to the teachings of Jesus received what the apostles received from Him. Without the close father/son relationship, those characteristics aren't necessarily passed on to the next spiritual generation.

Just as the natural son receives from his father's physical DNA, so does a spiritual son receive of his father's spiritual DNA. There will be a part of the father's anointing that flows down onto the son, due to their relationship. How well that flows down will depend a lot on how close their relationship is.

The prophet Elijah made an important statement about this to Elisha on his last day here on Earth, just before the chariot of fire took him up to heaven. The two had been traveling together, with Elijah going from one place to another and Elisha walking with him. Elisha refused to leave Elijah's side, even up to the very last, knowing that this would be the last day that they would be together.

How do I know that Elisha knew that? Because two different groups of prophets came to tell him so (2 Ki 2:3 & 5), and in both cases he responded, telling them that he knew (also 2 Ki 2:3 & 5). But that's not the important part. That comes next. The last conversation between Elijah and Elisha was:

> *And so it was, when they had crossed over, that Elijah said to Elisha, "Ask! What may I do for you, before I am taken away from you?" Elisha said, "Please let a double portion of your spirit be upon me."* [10] *So he said, "You have asked a hard thing. Nevertheless, if*

you see me when I am taken from you, it shall be so for you; but if not, it shall not be so."

(2 Kings 2:9-10)

"If you see me when I am taken from you." Doesn't sound like much of a requirement, does it? But that's because we're reading it through the lens of our culture. Elijah wasn't talking about seeing him from afar. The company of the prophets saw him taken up in the chariot of fire from afar, on the other side of the river. Yet they didn't receive anything. Only Elisha did. So, what was the difference?

What Elijah was saying would be better interpreted as "If you can stay eye to eye in agreement with me until I am taken from you."

When a child misbehaves, they won't look their parents in the eye. Likewise with someone in the church who speaks poorly about the pastor behind his back. Those who aren't in agreement can't really look you in the eye. They're ashamed. Being able to look someone in the eye conveys the idea "I'm with you." Elisha was clearly with Elijah, even though Elijah tested him, trying to get him to stay behind.

While the other prophets in the company were still prophets, they didn't receive what Elisha did. They weren't sons and Elijah wasn't their father. Only Elisha was in that relationship with Elijah, and so only he received the double portion.

How did the bond happen between Elijah and Elisha? How about the bond between Paul and Timothy? We don't really know. It was the same sort of bond of love that can happen between any two people, especially when God brings them together. They were family; not because of blood (other than the blood of Jesus); but because of the love they had for one another. The Holy Spirit had brought them together for a purpose, so that the father could impart into the son.

But there's something else important here; the idea of multiplication. Elisha asked for, and received a double portion of Elijah's spirit. We see this manifest in which twice the number of miracles are recorded in scripture from the ministry of Elisha, than are recorded during the ministry of Elijah. That's no accident. Elisha had clearly received something from his spiritual father.

When we allow the spiritual father/son relationship to play out to its fullness, we should see this sort of multiplication. Sadly, that has not been part of the church culture. It's something our spiritual ancestors lost along the way. But it can be brought back. We can do it. We can develop the kinds of relationships like Paul had with Timothy and Elijah had with Elisha and through them, reproduce spiritual sons who are more than we are, who go farther than we go, and who reach higher heights than we do.

In the closing of this chapter, I would like to leave you with these scriptures, along with a principle from them. 2 Kings 2:9-10 (Living Bible) *9* When they arrived on the other side Elijah said to Elisha, "What wish shall I grant you before I am taken away?" And Elisha replied, "Please grant me twice as much prophetic power as you have had."

> *¹⁰ "You have asked a hard thing," Elijah replied. "If you see me when I am taken from you, then you will get your request. But if not, then you won't."*

Shucks, here it is from v.10, The twenty-first century has given birth to what I want to call "an instant grits generation." They want what they want, and they want it right now. The text said, "when you see me" I likened that to a 440 relay in track. When one runner is passing the baton to another runner, they have what is called a "passing zone". I believe that this generation is trying to move too fast and not receiving the spiritual blessings (baton) from their Spiritual Father. They disconnect or drop the baton and go seek credentials to become an elder, pastor or bishop prematurely, only to discover that when they get the credentials, they had a bunch of zeal but not the knowledge they needed.

I also can see a problem with the principle of the older generation as it pertains to Spiritual Fathers who constantly, and consistently, year after year say their spiritual son or daughter is not ready for the next level. They selfishly want to hold onto their child a little longer, therefore they move slow and the prophetic mantle (baton) is not transferred in the "passing zone".

If we follow the pattern of scripture, spiritual fathers and mothers will not fail to impart to their spiritual sons and daughters the passion, purpose, and purity needed to finish the race. This is a word for both spiritual parents, and sons and daughters, to ensure that they are intersecting together in God's passing zone. Together they can win. Apart they will be disqualified.

The account of Moses' mentoring relationship with Joshua begins after the exodus from Egypt. Moses selected Joshua to lead the battle with Amalek (Exodus 17). Following this first mention, Joshua's name appears periodically in ways that indicate a close relationship with Moses.

Joshua was called Moses' minister and accompanied Moses to Mount Sinai (Exodus 24:13–14). He met Moses on his way down from the mountain (Exodus 32:17) and was called Moses' servant (Numbers 11:28). Joshua served as one of the spies chosen by Moses to go into Canaan and brought back a positive report (Numbers 13, 14).

God commanded Moses to position Joshua as his successor, which Moses did (Numbers 27:18, 22). Joshua was lifted up in the eyes of the people and succeeded Moses, leading the Israelites in the conquest of Canaan. Through these accounts, we witness Joshua fulfilling his destiny and Moses ensuring his legacy.

Success without a successor is actually failure. Though he did fail at times, Moses avoided failure by having a viable successor in the person of Joshua. He passed the baton to Joshua during his lifetime, ensuring that God's work would continue into a new generation. This is nowhere more evident than in his mentoring of young Joshua to become a great leader. The intergenerational connection between Moses and Joshua was critical to the successful passage of a new generation into the Promised Land. Time spent together, teaching by example, a life of integrity, the influence of blessing, and the power of positive words are all seen in this biblical model.

Like father, like son... only even more so.

Chapter 12

Tell Your Feelings How to Feel

Many people, regardless of age, long for spiritual fathers and mothers. If that's you, I want you to ask yourself why. Is it because no one has entered your life who is a spiritual mother or father? Or have you not made yourself available?

Take a moment right now, go somewhere quiet, and ask God to give you wisdom. James 1:5 says He promises to give us wisdom freely when we ask. Stand on that promise.

Now ask yourself: *Am I willing?*

Are you willing for somebody to speak into your life, to bring discipline and correction? You have to choose to be present, to open up your life to those around you. You can't be a one-man island and tough it out on your own. Our culture may tell you that you can be a rugged individualist and stand on your own two feet. The devil would love for you to think you can do that spiritually. But the truth is you need the influence of a spiritual parent.

The key for most men is being vulnerable. Psychologists tell us that men feel as many emotions as women do. However, men are good at hiding and suppressing them. We tell ourselves we shouldn't feel, but live by our wits and logic. We don't like to be vulnerable.

The truth is that a spiritual parent will say things that cut deeply. When your spiritual father or mother corrects you, it's going to *hurt*. I promise you that you might be tempted to disconnect from them and start searching for another set of spiritual parents. However, you will have those same feelings of toughing it out without them.

Shucks, those are just your feelings, and feelings are only indicators, not dictators. You must tell your feelings how to feel and not ask your feelings how they feel. Hello Somebody!

You may say, how can I control what I feel? Don't I just feel it without having any control? Remember, psychologists tell us that men have been teaching themselves to control their emotions for years. We just have to re-train ourselves in a different way. We don't need to be afraid of emotions. We must remember that one of the fruits of the Spirit is self-control. The Holy Spirit will help us grow in control in life — and that includes your emotions.

We have pointed out so many things that Paul has said,

but let me offer one more. This may have been some of the "harshness" we alluded to before in the lost letter to the Corinthians. He doesn't mince any words here in talking with the Galatians either:

> *You foolish Galatians! Who has bewitched you? Before your very eyes Jesus Christ was clearly portrayed as crucified. ² I would like to learn just one thing from you: Did you receive the Spirit by the works of the law, or by believing what you heard? ³ Are you so foolish? After beginning by means of the Spirit, are you now trying to finish by means of the flesh?*
>
> *(Galatians 3:1-5)*

Perhaps you remember times when your parents had to give you a harsh talking to and said, "This is going to hurt me more than it is going to hurt you!' Right?

I always doubted that until I became a parent. But when you are the person being taken to task, it is difficult. There is a mix of shame, guilt, humiliation, disappointment, and many other emotions. Sometimes you replay those feelings over and over again in their minds.

The devil likes to bring up those emotions as well. This is another area that the promise of self-control as a fruit of the Spirit comes in. God will help you when you are feeling this way to recognize the good in correction, and that it is done out of love.

It is natural when you feel as if you personally have the fight or flight response. We either get angry and defend ourselves or try to run and hide. That is as basic to all life on earth it seems as well. Even animals have this fight or flight response.

In the above passage, Paul was trying to get their attention loud and clear. It is like he is saying, did you forget what you clearly learned from the beginning? How could you be so foolish as to do that?

But isn't that human nature? We forget things that we don't remember and practice every day. The Galatians had done this. And it meant they were forgetting the very foundations of their faith.

Maybe we need to contrast the Galatians with someone Paul praised to bring the point home about constant input in our lives. Paul complimented the Berean Jews as more noble-minded than many others he visited because they were known for this:

> *[11]Now the Berean Jews were of more noble character than those in Thessalonica, for they received the message with great eagerness and examined the Scriptures every day to see if what Paul said was true.*
>
> *(Acts 17:11 New International Version)*

Notice two things that Paul compliments here as evidence of their noble character. First, is the Berean Jews' eagerness to receive the message of the gospel. Notice that eagerness is an attitude and perspective that goes beyond emotions. Certainly the good news of the gospel that Paul preached had the same cost of discipleship message that Paul preached elsewhere. They knew this message was a stumbling block to many, and Paul and many of his companions had suffered as a result. But they received the message eagerly.

The second is that they examined Scriptures daily to see and test that what Paul said was true. They loved Paul, but they knew that the Scriptures were infallible. Not Paul. Paul was God's messenger, but God's Word always took precedent.

The same should be true in how you approach the teaching of your spiritual parent — with eagerness — no matter what temporary pain that may lead to.

On one level, we know that many good things in life are painful. Try getting in shape when you have been out of it for a long time. Try overcoming obesity or addiction. There are times you are helpless in life on your own. There is pain involved as well, as you try to overcome what you feel like should just be a matter of you applying your will.

But there is pain that leads to good things, no matter how much it hurts at first. A mature response is to know that your spiritual parent's words are good for you — especially if it is coming from someone who loves you dearly and wants the best for you. So receive that word with eagerness.

Proverbs clearly tells us that "iron sharpens iron"

As iron sharpens iron, so one person sharpens another.

(Proverbs 27:17)

Think of your relationship as more of a trainer and trainee. Pick your favorite movie. Rocky may have been a world champion, but he had an amazing trainer and coach who took him there. Luke Skywalker had Yoda. The Karate Kid had Mister Miyagi. It is a way of learning that involves mistakes and pain.

Elisha willingly chose to go with Elijah, knowing how much it would cost. Elisha responded by sacrificing the team of oxen he had been plowing with. Elisha symbolically gave up everything he had known to that point.

Elisha also willingly followed even though he knew that Elijah was going to be whisked away from him. There is always a pain in the lessons of life. You will feel it in learning, but eventually you will also feel it in separation.

The companionship of a shared calling drove Elisha forward despite the pain in learning.

Look at Jesus in the Garden of Gethsemane:

> *"Father, if you are willing, take this cup from me; yet not my will, but yours be done."*
>
> *(Luke 22:42)*

Jesus faced his hour of truth just before His arrest. He wanted the cup to be removed because He knew how difficult it would be, but He wanted more, the Father's will to be accomplished.

Jesus poured out His emotions, but He did not let them deter Him from the task at hand. Jesus came to earth with this purpose in mind, and He was not going to back down. But, He was feeling the weight of what He was about to do.

Even in the midst of this moment, Jesus opened Himself up to the Father to pour into Him a message of confirmation in His mission. He was willing to submit to the Father's will. I ask again: are you willing?

Notice how Jesus submitting to the Father also was accompanied by His shepherding the disciples in the Garden. He brought them along, encouraged them to pray, chided them when they fell asleep, and then poured His heart out in prayer for them —

> *⁶ "I have revealed you to those whom you gave me out of the world. They were yours; you gave them to me and they have obeyed your word. ⁷ Now they know that everything you have given me comes from you. ⁸ For I gave them the words you gave me and they accepted them. They knew with certainty that I came from you, and they believed that you sent me. ⁹ I pray for them. I am not praying for the world, but for those you have given me, for they are yours. ¹⁰ All I have is yours, and all you have is mine. And glory has come to me through them. ¹¹ I will remain in the world no longer, but they are still in the world, and I am coming to you. Holy Father, protect them by the power of[b] your name, the name you gave me, so that they may be one as we are one. ¹² While I was with them, I protected them and kept them safe by that name you gave me. None has been lost except the one doomed to destruction so that Scripture would be fulfilled.*
>
> *¹³ "I am coming to you now, but I say these things while I am still in the world, so that they may have*

> *the full measure of my joy within them. ¹⁴ I have given them your word and the world has hated them, for they are not of the world any more than I am of the world. ¹⁵ My prayer is not that you take them out of the world but that you protect them from the evil one. ¹⁶ They are not of the world, even as I am not of it. ¹⁷ Sanctify them by the truth; your word is truth. ¹⁸ As you sent me into the world, I have sent them into the world. ¹⁹ For them I sanctify myself, that they too may be truly sanctified.*
>
> *(John 17:6-18)*

Amazing! Jesus prayed for them — their protection, their sanctification, their joy, and their recognition of being sojourners passing through this world. Now that is difficult for me to do when I am suffering. I am thinking about myself — Woe is me!

Even more amazing is how Jesus also prayed for us. Check this out!

> ²⁰ *"My prayer is not for them alone. I pray also for those who will believe in me through their message, ²¹ that all of them may be one, Father, just as you are in me and I am in you. May they also be in us so that the world may believe that you have sent me. ²² I have given them the glory that you gave me, that they may be one as we are one— ²³ I in them and you in me—so that they may be brought to complete unity. Then the world will know that you sent me and have loved them even as you have loved me.*
>
> *(John 17:20-23 (NIV)*

Jesus prayed for us — all those who believed as the result

of the message of the disciples. Jesus had the foresight to think of us in those moments as He prepared to give Himself as a sacrifice.

So that question is are you willing for your spiritual father to take you through the gauntlet of faith? The truth is, you will go through it anyway. Better someone to guide you through it who has your best interests in mind, even if it hurts at the moment. Someone who has gone through the gauntlet himself is helpful. Someone who knows the Jesus of the Garden is essential.

Quite often we hear people talk— from psychologists to playwrights and poets — about the struggle of living with your head or living with your heart. Understand it's not that you want to totally dismiss your emotions, but that you want your head to inform your emotions how you are going to act despite what you are feeling.

Many times, in the common language today, we talk about priorities for how we live our lives. Whether they are priorities, new year's resolutions, values, or your guiding principles or philosophy, they all have the same purpose in mind: you write down and agree what takes priority in your life and how you will respond to life's challenges *before* you get in a situation that will stress you.

The same principle is true in how parents today prepare their children for challenges they face. They talk about what is right and wrong, and how kids will respond in circumstances that will challenge their beliefs. They might even role play situations to give practical examples of what might happen. All of these things are meant to prepare kids for how they are going to respond when they are offered drugs or alcohol, tempted to lie or steal, and so on *before* it happens.

A spiritual father should guide you to set these type of priorities. For the pastor and other believers, this conversation should always start with what God has called you to do. What is your calling in life?

You should always take your feelings and put those up to the test of the Bible — like the Bereans. God will never call you to do something that disagrees with His Word. In fact, most of God's will for the lives of people are found in His Word and how He guides us to live, day in and day out. It's the other things that we have to seek God's will about and earnestly seek His direction.

A spiritual parent will help you work through those priorities so you can determine what's good for you and what's not, what fits your calling and what does not.

Many times you will find that there are also things in your life that are not bad or evil, but they are not the best for you. They waste your time or get your eyes off of your calling. This is where you can get your toes stepped on.

So you enjoy things that aren't bad but you justify wasting time on them when you could be investing that time with your family. Perhaps there are things you justify doing that aren't acting as a great witness. Listen to your spiritual parent and let his word — and the confirming conviction of the Holy Spirit — help you make the needed changes in your life.

Chapter 13

Never Expose Your Spiritual Parents

Our culture has a problem with social media. There is no doubt how addictive it can be, and it shapes how our youth think and view themselves. Often, that can be in a very negative way.

In the Fall of 2020, a new documentary was released called *The Social Dilemma*, which featured former executives of the social media companies blowing the whistle on something that happened. They created a way of getting people's attention in an addictive way — at first with the sole purpose of helping these individuals connect with others — but that quickly turned into a model for making money that created the firestorm we know social media can be today.

In a sense, these were children talking to the media about their "forefathers" in the industry — putting it out there for the whole world to see their dirty laundry. In all of that presentation, there was only one person who acknowledged taking the issues he saw to his company executives first. The rest aired their grievances to the world first, as far as we could tell.

Our culture has a tendency to question and distrust authority, making it as thought it is us against them. You see this exemplified by a general lack of respect in our culture.

Speaking of social media, you can see this general lack of respect every day in online videos. Social media has also fueled kids to performing everything from pranks and jokes to cruel and heartless acts for a laugh. The challenge can be attributed to a lack of respect in our culture. We don't know where the boundary lines are in our behavior because everything is seen and imitated.

Unfortunately, some people treat their parents or spiritual parents with disrespect as well — and that should never be the case — no matter how you are feeling or how you think you have been misunderstood.

Consider the following example from Genesis:

> *Noah, a man of the soil, proceeded to plant a vineyard. ²¹ When he drank some of its wine, he became drunk and lay uncovered inside his tent. ²² Ham, the father of Canaan, saw his father naked and told his two brothers outside. ²³ But Shem and Japheth took a garment and laid it across their shoulders; then they walked in backward and covered their father's naked body. Their faces were turned the other way so that they would not see their father naked.*

(Genesis 9:20-23)

What happened here? I think the most plain reading of this text is that Noah planted this vineyard, made wine, and had no idea the impacts of how much he drank of this new wine. He obviously had too much and passed out naked in his tent.

What did Ham do? Again, the most plain meaning is that Ham stumbled upon his father naked and drunk. He had a choice to make. Instead of grabbing something to cover his father up immediately, and ending this moment of shame, he ran to go get his brothers. Now why would he go do that?

We are not told Ham's demeanor. The classic painting "Drunkenness of Noah" obviously depicts Ham's demeanor as his brothers cover him up. Ham is not assisting his brothers but is amused by his drunk father's plight. This was the height of disrespect for Ham. Although the 10 Commandments had not been given at this point, "Honor your father and mother" by giving honor and respect toward parents was understood as what was expected. Ham obviously fell short.

Some try to reason that there had to have been something else that happened, even going as far as to guess that that Ham had a sexual encounter with Noah. That is unsupported by the text and simply not necessary to understand why Noah would pronounce a blessing on his other sons and a curse on Ham and his descendants.

It is enough disrespect to justify what Noah pronounced upon Ham. By his actions, Ham literally exposed Noah to the shame of telling others about his regretful situation and not taking care of his father as he should have by covering him up and protecting his decency.

You will find that your spiritual parents are not perfect either. They will make mistakes and expose themselves to the consequences of those mistakes. But the idea of you adding to their shame is beyond approach.

Paul had his share of disappointments in those who aided him but later fell away. Take Demas for example.

> *Demas has forsaken me, having loved this present world.*
>
> (2 Timothy 4:10)

Demas had been mentioned as a fellow laborer by Paul in his letter to Philemon. In the book of Colossians, Demas is with Paul as was Luke. But we see that his zeal and support for Paul did not last. Instead, his love for the world made him abandon Paul.

Consider Alexander the coppersmith as well. But notice Paul's clear message about how others should treat Alexander:

> *"14 Alexander the coppersmith did me much harm. May the Lord repay him according to his works. 15 You also must beware of him, for he has greatly resisted our words. 16 At my first defense no one stood with me, but all forsook me. May it not be charged against them."*
>
> (2 Timothy 4:14-16)

Perhaps these situations with Demas and Alexander reminded Paul of John Mark, the cousin of Barnabas who left them on their first missionary journey. However, many believe Mark left because of youth and immaturity. In any case, it is clear that Paul was not a "you turn your back on me, and I never speak to you again" kind of person. In fact, just after Paul tells Timothy about Demas, he asks Timothy to bring Mark to him because of his value to Paul. Paul clearly gave Mark a second chance. And certainly, Paul grieved over Demas.

That's loyalty, and you should be that loyal to your spiritual parent as well.

Even if the uncovering is the worst thing imaginable — a secret sin that compromises the ministry of your spiritual parent — the New Testament model involves you bring it up with your spiritual parent one-on-one.

> *If your brother or sister sins, go and point out their fault, just between the two of you. If they listen to you, you have won them over.*
> (Matthew 18:15)

But even in this church discipline process, the goal is to restore the sinner to a right relationship with God. It is never to shame or humiliate.

There would never be a reason to leave your spiritual parents exposed. Hang with them through thick and thin just as they would for you. You confront his understanding and do so in love. If you need to bring someone in to help him see the error of his ways, do so discretely and respectfully.

The trouble with our culture is that since the 1960s, we have been taught to question all authority in our culture. Our political leaders have often given us reason to do so.

But our culture has also given us the idea that every belief is correct in its own way. No one can criticize the other unless you are judgmental and intolerant. The truth is that you will face opposition and evil if you continue in the work of God.

> *Remember what I told you: "A servant is not greater than his master." If they persecuted me, they will persecute you also.*
>
> *(John 15:20)*

Paul taught this truth as well. In fact, Paul wrote about the benefit of suffering. He longed to "share in Christ's sufferings."

> *I want to know Christ--yes, to know the power of his resurrection and participation in his sufferings, becoming like him in his death.*
>
> *(Philippians 3:10)*

You need to be in a strong relationship with your mentor, recognizing that you will need each other as you face the opposition from this world. Build a relationship that is open and honest — where you can ask questions and even question why he believes something he does — but do so with respect and a willingness to learn. Be like

Mary who chose to sit at the feet of Jesus and listen:

> *Mary has chosen what is better, and it will not be taken away from her.*
>
> *(Luke 10:42)*

> *Jesus shared with Mary and Martha the mourning over the death of His friend and their brother, Lazarus. Death is perhaps the ultimate pain we face as we lose our beloved family and friends. It was in this time that "Jesus wept".*
>
> *(John 11:35)*

It was also during this time though, that these close followers of Jesus didn't understand. They were suffering. Their brother was dead. They said in their anguish, Jesus, "if you had been here, our brother would not have died" (John 11:21). Perhaps it was spoken in sorrow. Perhaps it was in blame.

But Jesus responded with the greatest truth that He perhaps had ever revealed:

> *I am the resurrection and the life. He who believes in Me, though he may die, he shall live.*
>
> *(John 11:25)*

There is great learning through suffering, and we see that shown to us through this story.

In a sense, our spiritual parents help us grow up and experience life how it really is – not how we hope it should be. Not avoiding hurtful things, but facing them head on.

Consider the following verses about spiritual maturity to encourage you.

> *When I was a child, I spoke like a child, I thought like a child, I reasoned like a child. When I became a man, I gave up childish ways.*
>
> *(1 Corinthians 13:11)*

Paul, in this context, is talking about love. Like so many in our culture, love may be equated with sex and not with the sacrificial love that God gives. We grow up in love as we know Him more and more each passing day.

> *For though by this time you ought to be teachers, you need someone to teach you again the basic principles of the oracles of God. You need milk, not solid food, for everyone who lives on milk is unskilled in the word of righteousness, since he is a child. But solid food is for the mature, for those who have their powers of discernment trained by constant practice to distinguish good from evil.*
>
> *(Hebrews 5:12-14)*

> *But I, brothers, could not address you as spiritual people, but as people of the flesh, as infants in Christ. I fed you with milk, not solid food, for you were not ready for it. And even now you are not yet ready, for you are still of the flesh.*
>
> *(1 Corinthians 3:1-2)*

Just like a baby grows from milk to soft food to solid food, we should grow in our ability to understand God's Word and live in godly wisdom — knowing how to apply God's Word to the circumstances of our lives.

> *Brothers, do not be children in your thinking. Be infants in evil, but in your thinking be mature.*
>
> *(1 Corinthians 14:20)*

Have a realistic view of your fallen nature and don't try to be good on your earn — as if you are earning salvation. Depend on Christ wholly for His righteousness.

> *And He gave the apostles, the prophets, the evangelists, the shepherds and teachers, to equip the saints for the work of ministry, for building up the body of Christ, until we all attain to the unity of the faith and of the knowledge of the Son of God, to mature manhood, to the measure of the stature of the fullness of Christ, so that we may no longer be children, tossed to and fro by the waves and carried about by every wind of doctrine, by human cunning, by craftiness in deceitful schemes.*
>
> *(Ephesians 4:11-14)*

This is the path of discipleship. It is all about growing to use our gifts to God's glory and help others develop their gifts to use in Christian service.

> *Do not be conformed to this world, but be transformed by the renewal of your mind, that by testing you may discern what is the will of God, what is good*

> *and acceptable and perfect.*
>
> *(Romans 12:2)*

Paul knew, even in his age, that the mind of Christ would run contrary to the mind of the world. Our mind is not just reformed, but transformed by Christ.

> *My little children, for whom I am again in the anguish of childbirth until Christ is formed in you!*
>
> *(Galatians 4:19)*

Paul equates spiritual parenting here to childbirth, longing for the day of maturity when Christ is fully formed in the life of the believer.

The truth in this chapter is about the fact that spiritual fathers bring a covering over you that frees you to serve God fully. It was never a relationship focused on control. He knows that your relationship with God is your responsibility alone.

But the sound thinking your spiritual parent gives you brings you protection that one person's life experience alone cannot. You will learn from your mistakes and your spiritual parent's advice.

Chapter 14

Never Divorce Your Spiritual Parents

There are several things in this world that are meant to be forever. We have talked about how God's love is eternal and everlasting. That is the key understanding of God's love as we have talked about in the Old Testament as well as the new. It is a faithful love that lasts until the end. The Christian knows that even if it is the end of life in this world, God and His love go on forever.

You should similarly think of your relationship with your spiritual parents the same way. You never "outgrow" them. Just like you never stop becoming a child of your parents, your bond with your spiritual parent will last. You must be faithful to it. Even after death, we can know that we will be united in the presence of Jesus for eternity. This bond as believers makes this relationship an eternal one.

But why do spiritual sons and daughters divorce spiritual parents? There are many reasons why this happens.

Sometimes people just make the wrong decision about their spiritual parents. Their lives are too busy in our fast-paced society today for people to stop and listen to God's voice. They may not really know why they need a spiritual father or what to look for in choosing one. That's part of the reason I wrote this book — to help people know how important spiritual fathers are and what to look for (and what to avoid) when choosing a spiritual father.

Sometimes people are just spiritually immature. That is a characteristic in these last days. The Bible tells us that people will have a form of the gospel without the power of God. People will draw spiritual leaders to themselves of people who speak words that only "tickle their ears." We are drawn to people who say what we want to hear, rather than face spiritual discipline. In the same way, people in our culture church hop to find the preacher that is pleasant, but never challenges them in ways it hurts and that they need for their growth.

Sometimes another spiritual father comes along with a bigger name or more numbers or dollars in their ministry. Some people jump from bandwagon to bandwagon, hoping to catch a shooting star rather than working to get there.

Let's face it. Sometimes spiritual fathers are also partially to blame, leaving for ministry opportunities or churches that come along. They are looking to go to the highest bidder. An example of this is found in Judges. A man named Micah happened to meet a young Levite, a priest who was looking for a place to settle. Micah made the Levite an offer he could not refuse.

> *Micah then said to him, "Dwell with me and be a father and a priest to me, and I will give you ten pieces of silver a year, a suit of clothes, and your maintenance." So the Levite went in.*
>
> *(Judges 17:10)*

There are several things about Micah we learn from this passage. He appears to have intentions to please God. Micah thinks after he hires the young Levite that "God will be good to me." But his heart is not fully turned to God — like so many of the kings to follow later in Israel's history. He cares deeply about his family's silver and uses part of this silver to pay the Levite. Micah even has an idol of silver that his family has personally set up to worship.

We learn much about the Levite too. We don't see him consider God in prayer when making the choice to stay with Micah. He has a place to stay, plus silver, provisions, and a new spiritual son through this deal.

But we see quickly that the Levite is soon persuaded to go to the highest bidder and take everything with him, too. The descendants of Dan are moving through as marauders, looking for a place to settle, and they make a similar offer to the Levite. They argue, "Isn't it better to be a priest to a whole tribe of Israel than one family?" It is an offer the Levite can't refuse, and he is gone. Micah is left behind in the dust.

Some call Paul the forsaken apostle because, even though he had so many loyal followers, he also had many who deserted him along the way. Paul writes to Timothy about one such experience.

> *15 You are aware of the fact that all who are in [the province of] Asia turned away and deserted me, Phygelus and Hermogenes among them. 16 The Lord grant mercy to the family of Onesiphorus, because he often refreshed me and showed me kindness [comforting and reviving me like fresh air] and he was not ashamed of my chains [for Christ's sake].*
>
> (2 Timothy 1:15-16 Amplified Bible)

Phygelus and Hermogenes turned out to be fair-weather friends. Nothing more is known about these two promising Christian leaders, who were evidently close to Paul but jumped ship when there later arose a personal cost of some sort.

Acutely aware and learned from what had happened previously with Phygelus and Hermogenes, in this passage Paul bespeaks and models a contrasting attitude to Timothy.

In the large context, Paul's message to Timothy is this: In times of trial, persecution, and betrayal, a strong disciple will not abandon the ship! He will refuse to equivocate, vacillate, or compromise on biblically clear matters, and he will not hesitate to speak the truth when necessary.

Implicit in the passage is that Paul did not want Timothy to go the way of Phygelus and Hermogenes in response to the pressures he was facing in leadership. There was no room in Paul's mind for a weak-kneed spiritual son. Paul cares for Timothy through examples, exhortations, reminders, and responsibility.

On the one hand, everyone in Asia abandoned Paul, including Phygelus and Hermogenes. Perhaps these two get mentioned because of how surprising it is that they abandoned Paul. Perhaps they were fellow-workers or spiritual sons with him in the gospel, and thus their abandonment cuts deep.

On the other hand, Onesiphorus not only stuck by Paul, but diligently searched for Paul in Rome in order to encourage and refresh him.

> *16 May the Lord show mercy to the household of Onesiphorus, because he often refreshed me and was not ashamed of my chains. 17 On the contrary, when he was in Rome, he searched hard for me until he found me. 18 May the Lord grant that he will find mercy from the Lord on that day! You know very well in how many ways he helped me in Ephesus.*
>
> *(2 Timothy 1:16-18)*

Onesiphorus was unashamed of Paul's chains. He didn't run from persecution and suffering but ran towards it because he wanted to serve Paul.

These examples are meant to embolden Timothy in his own ministry. Be like Onesiphorus. Don't run from the imprisoned apostle and the gospel of Jesus. Don't be like those who turn away from Christ's heralds in their moment of need. Paul cares for Timothy by holding up examples worth imitating and examples worth rejecting.

Timothy is not the only spiritual son he made an impassioned plea for. Paul makes an impassioned plea to Philemon on behalf of Onesimus in the letter we now know as the book of Philemon. Philemon is an interesting letter in that the entire book is basically Paul's impassioned plea on behalf of Onesimus.

> *"I appeal to you for my son Onesimus, who became my son while I was in chains."*
> *(Philemon 10 New International Version)*

Why was Paul so willing to speak up for Onesimus? We don't know the whole story behind Paul's letter, but we do know that Paul calls Onesimus a son, instead of a slave. We don't know how he found Paul, but Paul is clear to vouch for Onesimus based on his conversion and transformation as a believer.

Philemon must have had a relationship with Paul that was strong. Although Paul carefully treads in the case he makes for Onesimus, it is clear that he hangs the case on his personal relationship with Onesimus as a spiritual son. Onesimus is a believer that Paul has helped birth. This is not a "death row" conversion to Christianity to garner sympathy or a lighter judgment. Paul is vouching for Onesimus' belief.

Paul also vouches that Onesimus has been beneficial to Paul while he is in prison. In fact, Onesimus comes from a word that translates "beneficial." So Onesimus lived out his name in his relationship with Paul.

Paul suggests that now Onesimus can be useful to Philemon as well — not as a slave, but as a brother. Paul put his stamp of approval on Onesimus as his son. The book of Philemon has just turned into the best reference letter ever, written by a spiritual father about his son in the faith. Onesimus ministered to Paul as Onesiphorus did, when so many forsook Paul.

Let's go back to Elisha and Elijah once again. Elijah, it seems, always gave Elisha the space where he could have walked away from the relationship. From the very beginning, when Elisha asked to go back to this family first, Elijah didn't lay a guilt trip down on him. He knew it had to be Elisha's decision. And Elisha was not about to let this moment pass him by.

We see that Elisha never separated from his spiritual father until Elijah was caught up. This was true despite the fact that it looks like Elijah tried to send him away near the end. Elijah perhaps knew that all that they had experienced up until this point would be nothing like the stress Elisha would face here near the end as Elijah is taken away.

But this was the moment Elisha shined.

There is an old saying about a caterpillar transforming into a butterfly. You might feel sorry for it as it tries to push its way out of its chrysalis. But that moment of being strong enough to push its way out of its cocoon gives its wings the strength to fly. And that caterpillar transforms into a butterfly — and soars!

Elisha chose to face the difficult occasion of Elijah being taken from him. As we noted before, the journeys to the cities Elijah mentioned all references great moments of faith in God and God's faithfulness in return. Elisha experienced God's faithfulness that day when Elijah's mantle fell on him.

Your love is based on how God loved you. And his love is that faithful love.

Many people point to the book of Ruth as the Old Testament book that best illustrates the *haced* that we talked about before. Ruth, a Moabite woman (not a Hebrew), exemplified this love when she stayed with Naomi instead of leaving her as Orpah did. This is why these words of commitment spoken from a Moabite woman to her mother-in-law have traditionally been part of so many Christian wedding vows. These words are transformed in a Christian covenant marriage ceremony to symbolize the two becoming one flesh.

> *Ruth replied, "Don't urge me to leave you or to turn back from you. Where you go I will go, and where you stay I will stay. Your people will be my people and your God my God. ¹⁷ Where you die I will die, and there I will be buried. May the LORD deal with me, be it ever so severely, if even death separates you and me."*
>
> *(Ruth 1:16-17)*

Ruth followed Naomi back to Bethelehem and picked grains in the field for her to support them. Boaz noticed and responded in faithful love to Ruth as well, becoming Naomi's and Ruth's *goel* "kinsman redeemer" and securing her place in the lineage of King David and, ultimately, Jesus.

The gospel tells us that Christ loved us first, and we respond to Him because of His great love for us. The heart of the gospel message speaks of God's love in John 3:16. It makes us want to respond.

The heart of this chapter is that the bond between a spiritual father and son is a covenant relationship based on God's love. The spiritual father demonstrates that with great love for his spiritual son. You, as a spiritual son, should respond in that faithful way — like Onesiphorus and Onesimus for Paul, Elisha to Elijah, even Ruth for Naomi.

I used the term divorce in this chapter for a reason as well. This is another instance when an earthly concept teaches us a spiritual truth. The spiritual father and son relationship is a covenant relationship as is marriage. In our world where divorce is at least at 50% of all families — including believers — we just don't have a sense of how much God loves us and what a forever relationship means. But God shows us.

Consider God's love for the nation of Israel. He loved them even while they were in open rebellion against God. He loved them while they asked for another king to rule them. He loved them even while they were prostituting themselves with other idols and false gods. He sent prophets to remind them and call them back to repentance. Above all, God wanted a relationship with them.

God even sent Hosea as a message of hope and faithful love to the Israelites. Hosea acted out God's love for the people through his relationship with Gomer. Hosea continues to love Gomer faithfully to demonstrate how God loves His people despite their sin and idolatry:

> *Gomer[a] has many lovers, but you must continue loving her. Do this because it is an example of the* LORD's *love for Israel. He continues to love them.*
>
> (Hosea 3:1)

The New Covenant shows us an even more powerful example of God's faithful love. The fact that God sent Jesus to die for us was that fulfilling of God's covenant promise, His blood covenant with us.

It is amazing how life wears at us and the devil reminds us of our sin so often that we may forget God's love. We dwell on our mistakes as if we can negate God's love through a mistake or sin. But God's love is truly powerful. Nothing can separate us from His love. Pauls' words about God's love may be the most powerful reminder of that we could have.

> [35] *Who shall separate us from the love of Christ? Shall trouble or hardship or persecution or famine or nakedness or danger or sword?* [36] *As it is written:*
>
> *"For your sake we face death all day long; we are considered as sheep to be slaughtered."*[a]

> *37 No, in all these things we are more than conquerors through him who loved us. 38 For I am convinced that neither death nor life, neither angels nor demons,[b] neither the present nor the future, nor any powers, 39 neither height nor depth, nor anything else in all creation, will be able to separate us from the love of God that is in Christ Jesus our Lord.*
>
> *(Romans 8:35-39)*

The truth throughout this chapter is that spiritual fathers provide a safe environment of love that empowers you to continue loving even in the worst of times. You feel safe in their presence because of how much they love you. This equips you to love in an uncommonly strong way when you are surrounded by those who love you like God loves you.

God will not divorce you, so you should follow His example of love and never divorce your spiritual parents.

It's About Legacy

Let's conclude with something you have not thought about as a spiritual son. Your spiritual parent is fulfilled through this relationship with you. That's right – you are a spiritual heritage for them in a way that children are for parents.

Psychologists tell us that one of the central concerns of senior adults is about the legacy they are leaving behind — whether that is a monetary inheritance, their children and grandchildren, or their spiritual legacy for the kingdom of God. You are part of their legacy.

Consider the following ways to honor your spiritual parents:

1. Involve them in the milestone events of your family.

This includes anniversaries, birthdays, graduations, concerts, ball games, and certainly events like baptisms and dedications. Your spiritual parents become part of your family in a way that you might treat parents or grandparents, aunts or uncles.

2. Take time to thank them regularly.

Put this on your calendar if you need to. At least, add their birthday and anniversary to your calendar. Consider sending a gift each Father's or Mother's Day. In the history of the church, All Saints Day on November 1 is the day you honored special saints in your life as well. So, whatever makes the most sense for you, pour out your thanks to them.

3. Share what God is teaching you regularly.

The tendency in a longtime relationship will be to talk about issues and challenges as they arise. As men, you sometimes will turn into problem-solving mode as well. You will focus on what you can solve rather than what you are learning. This will also hold you accountable to remaining in God's Word and prayer regularly.

4. Schedule a time to participate in their ministry.

We spoke earlier about giving money, but also find that one time a year when you can be part of his ministry as well. Be a smiling face in the crowd that takes your mentor by surprise. Do this even if it means traveling a little extra to get there.

5. Journal what you have learned from your spiritual parents and present it to them

If you like to write, go with the journal. If you don't, make a bulleted list of the things you learned. Either one will be valuable feedback to your parent and a reminder to you of how your spiritual parent and God have been faithful to you.

Through doing these things, your spiritual parent will be blessed and a blessing to you through these life events. My wife and I have been spiritual son and daughter to our spiritual parents for 25 consistently. Yes, unbroken covenant! In fact while I was writing this book I cried several times because I have watched people walk in and out of their lives for years know matter how much my spiritual parents imparted and loved them, yet they still left and I watched them still preach during the stormy days of ministry.

I've learned by observing my spiritual parents and that there are so many people with agendas (as well as cocky, flaky, biblically-unbalanced people) lurking out there who are trying to use their brand as a stepping stone to promote themselves. Because of that it has caused my spiritual parents to become very insulated, and you can't get near their hearts as quickly as others have in time past. They do this to protect themselves. Unfortunately, it is a necessary factor given how many agenda-driven people exist in our churches today.

The bottom line is that it is virtually impossible to gain relational access to high level leaders because of this hurt and betrayal. It has now to be a God-thing and now sons and daughters must prove themselves. I must confess that I'm very protective of my spiritual parents because of what I have observed. Maybe that's not a good thing, but it is what it is.

Smile, reflection moment, I can remember in 2020 that my spiritual parents came to talk to my wife and I about some things. Boom out of nowhere dad ask me how much money we had in the bank and I responded, are you talking about the church account or our personal account? He said, your personal account. I said I don't know dad, baby tell dad how much we have in the account. She gave him the amount, he said okay and we started talking about other things.

After both of them got finished putting the rod of correction on us we went out to eat at the Brazilian restaurant in Jacksonville. While my wife and I were driving they were following us in their own vehicle and I just burst out laughing. If dad would have asked me that question when I was in my 20's I'm like cool, but here I am a grown-behind man in my 50's, retired from the United States Army, three biological children, a son-in law and a grandchild and now you want to ask me a question like that.

Welp, that is what it's all about, transparency before your spiritual parents while remaining connected. Having a spiritual father is simply a concept that God illustrates through the Bible for mankind to have a pattern to follow in His ways. The Word of God does not teach that people need to earn acceptance from a human spiritual father, but it does illustrate how spiritual sons pursued their leaders as spiritual fathers in efforts to receive what they had from God.

Elisha and Timothy are great examples in their humble submission to their leaders, not to earn acceptance but to gain God's approval to do the work by learning through their leaders. One of the greatest benefits of being around a spiritual father is they help provide sanity and sound thinking by what they share, demonstrate and advise. At the end of the day, you know they have your back, so this empowers you in your own growth and ministry.

They often battle many things that you don't have to battle, so we can learn from their trials. We'll have to face our own trials, but we become encouraged to walk through those trials with greater confidence.

Spiritual fathers help you gain empowerment to work in your sphere of influence. Their covering provides, wisdom, interaction and healthy warnings. As Paul said, *I do not write these things to shame you, but as my beloved children I warn you.* (1 Corinthians 4:14). Sometimes after they are done talking, you'll need some time alone to process what they just said and how deep it hit your heart. Their view of God and walk with Him cause you to make changes in your own life after experiencing the weight of what they say.

> *¹ My dear brothers and sisters, it's obvious that our ministry among you has proven to be fruitful.*
>
> *² And though we had already suffered greatly in Philippi, where we were shamefully mistreated, we were emboldened by faith in our God to fearlessly preach his wonderful gospel to you in spite of incredible opposition.*
>
> *³ Our coming alongside you to encourage you was not out of some delusion, or impure motive, or an intention to mislead you, ⁴ but we have been approved by God to be those who preach the gospel. So our motivation to preach is not pleasing people but pleasing God, who thoroughly examines our hearts. ⁵ God is our witness that when we came to encourage you, we never once used cunning compliments as a pretext for greed, ⁶ nor did we crave the praises of men, whether you or others.*
>
> *⁷ Even though we could have imposed upon you our demands as apostles of Christ, instead we showed you kindness and were gentle among you. We cared for you in the same way a nursing mother cares for her own children. ⁸ With a mother's love and affectionate attachment to you, we were very happy to share with you not only the gospel of God but also our lives—because you had become so dear to us.*
>
> *⁹ Beloved brothers and sisters, surely you remember how hard we labored among you. We worked night and day so that we would not become a burden to*

you while we preached the wonderful gospel of God. ⁱ⁰ With God as our witness you saw how we lived among you—in holiness, in godly relationships, and without fault. ¹¹ And you know how affectionately we treated each one of you, like a loving father cares for his own children. ¹² We comforted and encouraged you and challenged you to adopt a lifestyle worthy of God, who invites you into his kingdom and glory.

(1 Thessalonians 2:1-12 The Passion Translation)

These words I leave with you, and I pray that your quest to find your own Spiritual son, daughter, or parent is fruitful, and that the wisdom you learn from the relationship blesses you for all your days. Please remember that Spiritual and moral life is not taught in the classroom; it is learned in the laboratory of life. Many leaders today can, when questioned, give a long laundry list of men and women who's influenced their lives, but these same leaders cannot point to a spiritual mother and father in ministry and it's time for a change. #Shucks

www.ingramcontent.com/pod-product-compliance
Lightning Source LLC
Chambersburg PA
CBHW071855160426
43209CB00005B/1067